If you think God retired after the New Testament, read a few of these testimonies! In this series, Melanie Hemry and Gina Lynnes share the true stories of believers, just like you, who have run into all kinds of tragedies and come out on the winning side—and their amazing testimonies will show you that miracles are still happening today!

Melanie Hemry is a gifted writer whom I've known for many years. She coauthored this series because she knows, like I do, that anyone who has the gall and audacity to *obey* and *believe* God's Word can see His power in his or her life.

God bless you as you read and may God's amazing energy and power flow through you!

—*Dr. Jesse Duplantis*
Jesse Duplantis Ministries

Jesus said if you know the truth, the truth will set you free. In this book, Melanie and Gina have presented the truth in a way that makes it fun and easy to understand. Their stories will fill you with faith, hope and love. So get comfortable and prepare to receive the anointing that will destroy every yoke and remove every burden in your life.

—*Mylon and Christi Le Fevre*
Mylon Le Fevre Ministries

GOD'S POWER
for
CHILDREN

GOD'S POWER

for

CHILDREN

Melanie Hemry & Gina Lynnes

WHITAKER
HOUSE

GOD'S POWER FOR CHILDREN

(Previously published as *Anointing for Children*)

ISBN: 978-1-60374-920-6
eBook ISBN: 978-1-60374-921-3
Printed in the United States of America
© 2007, 2013 by Melanie Hemry and Gina Lynnes

Whitaker House
1030 Hunt Valley Circle
New Kensington, PA 15068
www.whitakerhouse.com

Library of Congress Cataloging-in-Publication Data (Pending)

1 2 3 4 5 6 7 8 9 10 ⊔⊔ 19 18 17 16 15 14 13

DEDICATION

This book is respectfully dedicated to the heroic Christian mothers and fathers whose children departed this life too early and are now awaiting the joyful reunion that will one day take place in the glory of heaven's sweet light. We have known such parents and have been awed to see them find a source of comfort and strength in God that is nothing short of miraculous. We have watched them rise from the ashes of life's greatest anguish and light up the lives of others with a brilliance unique to those who have experienced that kind of emotional resurrection. They deserve our most profound respect.

May God continue to grant all of us revelation from His Word so that more parents can be spared such loss. And may those of us who are spared it, and have the opportunity to see our children's children, have the grace to praise God as faithfully in our joy as those who missed that opportunity have praised Him in the midst of their pain.

You will always be an inspiration to us.

CONTENTS

Part One

THE ARROWS
OF THE ALMIGHTY

By Gina

Part One

THE ARROWS
OF THE ALMIGHTY

*Like arrows in the hand of a warrior, so are the children
of one's youth. Happy is the man who has his quiver full of
them; they shall not be ashamed, but shall speak with their
enemies in the gate.*
—Psalm 127:4–5

She stood alone in the shadows of the sanctuary for some time
before I saw her, twisting a damp handkerchief and gathering
the courage to share her story. The women's conference over, the
other ladies had already drifted out to the foyer, laughing and
chatting, their heels clicking happy rhythms on the linoleum tile
as they went. Only the folded paper fans that fluttered earlier in
their hands as they fought to stay cool despite the summer heat
remained, strewn here and there on the empty metal chairs.

As I gathered my notes and Bible, the crunch of tires rolling across the gravel outside echoed in through the windows. The parking lot would be desolate soon. Few women were brave or foolish enough to linger after dark in this part of the city. Hurrying to join the caravan, I thought of the teenagers I'd seen earlier, slouched against deserted store-fronts, snarling curses at passing cars. *Better leave before it gets too late.*

She caught my eye as I turned toward the door. An ebony beauty in a black and white dress, she was still pressed and perfect even in the wilting heat. At first glance only the wrinkled handkerchief hinted at her sorrow. But when I reached out to take her hand, she clutched my fingers as if they were a lifeline and drew herself into my arms.

"If I had only known sooner," she cried. "What you showed us tonight in the Bible about prayer and God's promises for our children, if I'd only known it before, I might have been able to help him."

Over the next few moments, her story tumbled out in sob-wracked phrases. *A teenage son. A good boy, really. Just involved with the wrong people. Shot dead in a gang fight. Murdered in the street the previous summer.*

There was no bitterness in her voice as she told me about it; no blaming of God for the loss she had suffered, just an aching emptiness only the Almighty Himself could fill. Hugging her to myself, I prayed that He would do so. Then we rested our heads on each other's shoulders and cried.

I never saw that precious mother again, but our encounter left a permanent mark on my heart. Her tears inspired in me the determination to tell the story of my own son; to share how I discovered the truth about the divine power that we, as believers, can release in the lives of our children. As I learned by painful experience when it was almost too late, that power not only can protect our sons and daughters, it can help us raise them wisely and send them forth as flaming arrows of righteousness to light up a darkened world.

In this troubled age, such a thing might sound impossible... but I know from experience that's what God's promise of protection for our children can do.

A Teenager in Tornado Alley

Unlike the son who lived his short life and lost it on the inner city streets, my son, Aaron, stumbled into danger in the peaceful, suburban neighborhoods of Edmond, Oklahoma. No one would have ever called Edmond a violent place. In a town peppered with parks and scattered with shiny school buildings and churches of every variety, the only evil Edmonites expected to see in their community was the kind that, from March through September, stabbed at them from the sky with dark, funnel-shaped fingers.

But they were used to that kind of danger. Just as mothers in the inner cities dragged their youngsters into the house at the sound of gunshots and squealing tires, Edmond moms dragged their kids into the hallways when the tornado sirens blared. That's just what you do when you live in the part of the country known as Tornado Alley.

The first spring our family lived in Edmond, we hunkered down in the hallway so many times I lost count. It didn't bother me, though; I'd grown up in Tornado Alley. I understood how quickly storms could erupt and how devastating they could be, but I also knew how to watch for them. I learned as a kid what it meant when a gust of cool wind shuddered through a warm, spring afternoon. I knew to keep a sharp eye on the clouds when they churned bluish green and flexed their muscles on the horizon.

I only wish I'd been as alert to the storm that gathered on Aaron's horizon during the spring of his senior year; but even the most well-meaning mothers sometimes miss the first signs of trouble. So when the phone rang on that sunny March afternoon, I didn't hear the low rumble of spiritual thunder behind it. I didn't notice the brief chill that swept over my heart. All I heard was the lilting accent of my son's elderly French teacher.

"Halloo, thees ees Madame Dubois. I am speaking weeth Aaron's mama, yes?"

"Yes, I'm Aaron's mother. Is there something I can do for you?"

"I am calling to ensure that you know Aaron is failing my class. He is a smart boy and I tell him all the time, '*Baby*—I call all of my students *baby*—if you will just come to class, you will do well. But how can you pass if you are all the time absent?' I am thinking that as his mother, you can help him attend more often."

I hesitated, struggling to sort out my confusion. "Absent? Aaron is absent?" I answered. "No...no, that's a mistake. He goes to school every day. Never misses. And he's always been a good student."

Her voice stubbornly polite, Madam Dubois plunged on. "If you'll pardon me, please, I think he does come to school. But then sometimes he leaves to smoke with the other boys."

"Smoke? Aaron's not a smoker!" I said. "Even if he wanted to hang out with boys who smoked, why would they leave the school campus?"

Madam Dubois interrupted. "Whatever the reason for his absences, they are causing him to fail French," she said, "and I would think he needs the credits to get his diploma in May."

Thanking Madame Dubois for the information, I hung up the phone and stared at it as if it had momentarily sprung to life and tap-danced on my desk. The entire conversation mystified me. Not only did my gentle, quiet son bring home report cards brimming with As and Bs, for the past several years he'd spent hours after class in the school auditorium rehearsing for extra-curricular musicals and dramatic productions. If anything, Aaron spent too much time at school—not too little.

The whole idea of him skulking around with a pack of ne'er-do-wells, sucking on cigarettes and cutting classes was preposterous. Why on earth would he do such a thing?

If I had only paid attention to that question, things might not have happened as they did. If I had only asked the Lord at the very beginning for His wisdom, I could have averted great heartache. But I was too spiritually naive to realize then how subtle the forces of darkness can be; and I assumed that because I loved the Lord and took my children to church, everything in their lives would automatically turn out all right. Certainly I had read the warning in the Bible about being alert and vigilant, because *"your adversary the devil walks about like a roaring lion, seeking whom he may devour"* (1 Peter 5:8). I knew the New Testament commands us to *"resist him, steadfast in the faith"* (verse 9). But I hadn't even begun to grasp the gravity of those words. It never occurred to me that the devil himself was circling my son, plotting his destruction.

As a result, the seriousness of Madame Dubois' observations slipped past me like a cat darting unseen into the house when the screen door swings open. Come to think of it, Aaron had mentioned she was strange. He said she was a member of the French resistance during World War II and joked that the stress of it left her slightly deranged.

I thought he was kidding. Maybe he wasn't.

Sounding the Alarm

Some kinds of weather are forthright and honest. They march across the map like meteorological armies bringing predictable, through sometimes dramatic, changes. If such a front is headed your way and you want to know what to expect, just tune in to the Weather Channel and you can find out. Some kinds of weather-makers are convenient that way; tornadoes are not.

Tornadoes are like the devil; they sneak up on you. If you don't stay alert, they can be on you before you know it. When tornadoes are about, a smiling afternoon can roil into a rage and splinter whole neighborhoods in seconds, scattering their shreds like matchsticks in every direction. I'd seen just such a neighborhood when our family first moved to Edmond. Driving around, looking for a place to live, we came upon it unexpectedly. What a shock it was to see, right in the midst of the city, a few blocks of flattened lumber and battered belongings where homes had once stood.

I wondered, looking at the devastation, if the people who lived there had been warned. Had they heard the tornado sirens and taken cover? Or had they been caught unaware, never having seen it coming?

I can never blame God for failing to warn me of the spiritual storm that blew in during Aaron's seventeenth year. When the winds first kicked up, the Holy Spirit sounded the alarm. I first sensed it late one Friday night, a few weeks after the French teacher's peculiar call. My older son, Christopher, and my daughter, Jennifer, were already asleep in their rooms. Aaron was out with some friends but I knew he'd be home soon, so, exhausted from the day, I fell into bed.

Once there, however, I couldn't rest. Plagued by some unexplainable anxiety, I wrestled with the sheets and pummeled my pillow while one relentless thought pestered me.

Aaron is not where he said he would be.

I can't recall now exactly where Aaron had professed to be going that evening. Whatever the story, it had given me no cause for concern. *But what if he isn't there?* I wondered. *Where could he be?*

I knew the answer immediately. It wafted into my mind like the distant sound of a storm siren set off by mistake on a clear day. *Aaron is partying tonight with people you don't know...and he has been drinking.*

Hours later when Aaron tiptoed through the front door in the early morning, he found me waiting for him with arms crossed and jaw clenched. I confronted him with what I felt the Holy Spirit had revealed to me, secretly hoping I was wrong. I wasn't. My son had indeed been drinking. Instead of fueling my indignation by lying about it, he bowed his head in regret, admitted the truth, and accepted the consequences without argument. "I'm sorry, Mom," he said as he disappeared into his room. "I'm so sorry."

For the next few hours, I sat alone in the dark wondering what was happening. Surely, I thought, this is just a one-time event. Boyish curiosity. Youthful lack of judgment. Nothing more.

Please God, don't let it be anything more.

Such was the pitiful, inadequate prayer I prayed. I realized months later, it was not even a prayer at all—just a wish that, without the force of faith to propel it heavenward, drifted to the ground as soon as it was uttered, accomplishing nothing.

Miracles and Messy Rooms

If Madame Dubois' phone call was the first gust of wind, Aaron's Friday night escapade was the first lightning flash on the horizon. But I missed them both because Aaron had always been such a sunny child. Ever since he sloshed his way into the baptistery as a little boy, he'd loved going to church. Along with rock stars and pro athletes, his heroes included fiery preachers who delivered the Word with power. When such a preacher held a meeting, Aaron wasn't above breaking into a run to claim a seat in the front row. He was always happiest where the anointing was strong and the spit was flying.

By the time he hit high school, he was so full of confidence in the miracle-working power of God that on his sixteenth birthday he made just one request. He asked our family to lay hands on him and pray for him to grow taller. At 5'2", he was tired of being the shortest kid in the choir photos. We all knew that, given his genes, the odds were against him. Most of his relatives on his father's side topped out at about five and a half feet. Some stood on tiptoe to hit that mark. But we prayed and Aaron believed.

Initially, I figured that prayer would be an inexpensive birthday present. I figured wrong. Buying new blue jeans every month for a kid who is shooting skyward as fast as Jack's beanstalk costs plenty, but we had no other choice. By his seventeenth birthday, Aaron stood almost six feet tall.

Of course, his messy room, his refusal to respond to his alarm clock every morning, and—once he began to drive—the unpaid traffic tickets stuffed in the glove compartment of his car still qualified him as a normal, teenage boy. But through it all, I clung confidently to a prophecy taped to his bedroom wall that was written to him by his cousin when they were both in elementary school. It said, "Just keep walking with Me, says the Lord, and I will lift you up to become a great blessing to My people."

Granted, it was a simple word declared by one child to another; but it rang true and I assumed it would easily come to pass. After all, I'd prayed over each of my three children for years the words from Philippians 2:15–16, asking God to help them be:

*blameless and guileless, innocent and uncontaminated, chil-
dren of God without blemish (faultless, unrebukable) in the
midst of a crooked and wicked generation...among whom you
are seen as bright lights (stars or beacons shining out clearly) in
the [dark] world, holding out [to it] and offering [to all men]
the Word of Life.* (AMP)

I knew God had heard me every time I prayed those words.
But I failed to take into account the fact that the devil had heard
me, too.

In This World You Will Have Trouble

I wish every Christian parent could learn early what I learned
when it was almost too late—that if you want your children to
fulfill their destiny in the kingdom of God, you'll have to fight the
good fight of faith over them. You'll have to follow the instructions the apostle Paul wrote to an up-and-coming young minister
two thousand years ago. *"This charge I commit to you, son Timothy,
according to the prophecies previously made concerning you, that by
them you may wage the good warfare"* (1 Timothy 1:18).

Even if you're the perfect parent (which, of course, nobody but
God Himself actually is), even if you take advantage of every wonderful parenting class your church offers, some evil will eventually worm its way into your little garden of Eden. Some serpent
of rejection or temptation will strike at your children, and when it
does, you will have to fight for them on your knees. Wielding the
promises of Scripture like a sword, you'll have to slash to shreds
every demonic thing that attacks your kids.

Jesus Himself said, *"In this world you will have trouble"*
(John 16:33 NIV). For Aaron, that trouble came from every
side. It erupted first at school when the director of the fine arts

department, his rage veiled beneath a thin veneer of control, called Aaron into his office and accused him of stealing.

Stunned and humiliated, Aaron maintained his innocence. "What on earth would make you think I'd do such a thing?" he asked. Another student had identified him as the thief, he was told. Just admit the truth and all would be forgiven. But Aaron refused to confess to a crime he did not commit, and his refusal stoked the director's fury.

Shamed in front of his fellow students and blacklisted by the drama director, Aaron wandered bewildered through the next few months. He had spent years working on his vocal and acting talents. As a sophomore and junior, he'd landed major roles in every school production. But now as a senior—in this most important high school year—he found himself locked out of the plays and musicals that had always been his passion. He struggled to overcome the prejudice by practicing extra hours for his auditions. But no matter; when the casting sheet was posted and the contenders crowded around to see who'd been granted the coveted roles, Aaron's name was missing from the list.

As if that wasn't enough, one day after school a burly athlete with a chip on his shoulder found his car damaged and, again, somebody fired off a rumor that Aaron was the culprit. It was a lie; but it took root among a rough crowd that vowed retribution. From then on, their threats of violence stalked Aaron not only in the school hallways but at home. One morning, he stepped out our front door heading for school to find his car windows smashed and our lawn scarred by tire tracks, the sod chewed into chunks.

"Aaron," I said, surveying the damage, "why on earth would somebody do such a thing?"

He just shrugged. Embarrassed by the accusations and ashamed of his own fears and seeming failures, he stayed silent as his world turned upside down. At seventeen years old, he was too much of a man to come running to his mother for help.

Had I known then what I know now, I would have turned immediately to the Lord for counsel. I would have taken Him up on the promise He gave us in James 1:5: *"If any of you lacks wisdom, let him ask of God, who gives to all liberally and without reproach, and it will be given to him."*

God alone knows the secrets of our children's hearts. He understands the pain they feel and the struggles they face better than we, as natural parents, ever could. He also knows in advance the strategies the devil plans to use against them. If we will ask Him in faith, He will show us exactly what is happening and what we should do. He will enable us to guide our children to safety before the storms of life cause them harm.

Ask God for help. That seems like such an obvious thing to do. In the years since, I've done it many times and spared my children major calamities. But back then, I didn't know how to do that. So I just kept loving my son and hoping for the best.

Aaron's a good boy, I told myself. *The drama director and the kids at school will soon see that and then this mess will blow over.*

It blew over, all right. But by the time it did, there was virtually nothing left of the son I'd once known.

The Day the Tornado Touched Down

Aaron staggered, wounded, through his senior year at high school. Cut off from his familiar friends at school, he sought the company of the smokers Madame Dubois had warned me about. He even buddied up with an active member of the Crips gang he met while working part-time on the maintenance crew at church. He knew those people weren't good for him, but their companionship filled the empty hours once occupied with play rehearsals and ensemble practices. And their tough reputation offered some protection from the windshield-smashing delinquents who threatened him.

Despite his shadowy friends, however, Aaron still loved being a part of the youth group at church. It was the only place besides home he felt safe and happy.

That changed the day the youth pastor called him into his office and told him he'd heard about his new friends. "You're a negative influence on the youth of this church, Aaron," he said. "I don't want you around anymore."

No doubt, from the youth pastor's perspective, the situation seemed simple. Aaron was a Christian boy from a good family who was misbehaving. What he needed was a sharp rebuke to straighten him up. We've all made misjudgments like that. We've all harbored the idea that, like God, we can see down into someone's soul, identify what's wrong, and fix it with an authoritative whack from our scriptural hammer. When we do that, we often break the fragile vessel we intended to mend because there's almost always something we don't know.

What the youth pastor didn't know about Aaron that day could fill volumes. He didn't know that Aaron's natural father had taken off many years before and that he'd never recovered from the loss. He didn't know that as a five-year-old boy, Aaron had crumbled, shaking and frightened beneath the wrath of man he wanted desperately to please—a man who ever after mocked and belittled him—and that he'd hungered ever since for a man he respected to affirm him. He didn't know that Aaron had spent his whole life admiring ministers and that to be rejected by one was the cruelest blow he could imagine.

He'd just heard that Aaron was smoking cigarettes with the wrong kind of people...and he assumed that's all he needed to know.

A Ticking Time Bomb

The day his youth pastor rejected him was the day the tornado touched down in Aaron's life, swooping down in a swirl of fury and a darkness I couldn't comprehend. Overnight, torrents of angry rap music swept away the Broadway tunes he'd sung and played during his high school production years. The dark winds of Metallica and Alice in Chains replaced his once-beloved Christian rock. His hair mutated into unlikely shapes and colors. Mohawks and mullets, in angry shades unknown to nature, shouted at me about something; but for the life of me, I couldn't make out what they were saying.

Since Aaron never disclosed what the youth pastor had said, I could only assume he was just passing through a phase. Surely, he wouldn't go through his entire life with a green Mohawk and playing air guitar to Metallica's *Black Album*. I considered just laying down the law; using the oft-quoted parental line about living under my roof and abiding by my rules. *Shape up or get out*, I was tempted to say. But something in his eyes stopped me. When I looked beyond the rebellious glint, it seemed I could see hiding behind it a boy so wounded that one more blow of rejection would finish him off.

Desperate and confused, I tried to figure out what had gone wrong, but I couldn't. One day as I drove the streets of Edmond, I found myself pounding the steering wheel, tears streaming down my face, asking the question I should have asked in the very beginning. "Lord, why?" I called out, not really expecting an answer. "Why has all this happened to Aaron? He's just a boy—a sweet, harmless boy!"

Reverberating from my spirit came a divine reply that permanently altered my perspective. *To the devil, Aaron is more than just a boy. He is a child of the righteous who has been taught My Word and filled with My Spirit. He is a ticking time bomb with the potential to do great damage to the kingdom of darkness, and the devil is frantic to destroy him before that bomb goes off.*

That's when I realized the deadly nature of the spiritual battle that rages over the children of believers. That's when I knew that if I wanted to win this battle, I would have to do more than lob spiritual S.O.S. signals toward the sky and cry myself to sleep wondering if help would ever come. I would have to learn how to use the spiritual weapons God had given me. I would have to learn how to fight.

For a while, I rose up full of determination and confidence. Then I got the news. Due to a job transfer, our family would soon be moving from Edmond to Denver. Aaron, having graduated from high school, decided he was old enough now to go his own way. He would not be going with us. The day I hugged him goodbye, I felt like I was setting him adrift alone on a fragile raft in the middle of some vast, shoreless ocean. Driving north on I-35, with every mile that passed I felt him slip further beyond my reach until the distance swallowed him up, and he was gone.

How will I ever help him now? I wondered. *How will he ever find his way home?*

Don't Mess with an Angry Mother

It was years before I learned the details of the lifestyle my son sank into once he was on his own. Drug parties stretched for days and nights on end. The same boy who once perched on the edge of a front row seat in believers' meetings spent his weekends slouched in drug houses or lingering in parking lots smoking marijuana, dropping acid, or snorting cocaine. Within months, he found himself homeless and jobless. Singing vocals with a no-name rock band and hanging out in bars all night, he slept his days away in the apartment of his old friend from the Crips gang—the only person who would take him in.

The drug-induced fog he lived in obscured, for the most part, the danger that surrounded him; but occasionally it slashed through the haze like a switchblade wielded by some unseen hand. He saw its glint one night when a pickup truck driven by angry men with a score to settle mowed down one of his drug buddies before his very eyes. Even the chemicals in his bloodstream couldn't soften the shock of seeing his friend slammed onto the hood of the truck and hurled headfirst against the curb.

For a few hours, the sharp edge of reality startled Aaron to his senses. The sight of an open skull and the streams of blood flowing from it onto the pavement...the shrieking ambulance sirens... the wind slapping his face as he rode his friend's motorcycle to the emergency room amid the flashing lights of a police escort... reminded him just how deadly this lifestyle might be. But then the fog settled in again. The dangers seemed to dissipate, and he went on as before.

At the time, I knew none of this. Aaron rarely called me after we moved. I usually didn't even know where he was. For all practical purposes, my son had vanished.

I continued to search the Bible to see what it had to say about the children of believers and prayed for him every day. But the more I prayed, the more I sensed that death itself was stalking him, creeping closer all the time. Eventually, the urgency within me increased until I could almost see the devil's twisted fingers holding a gun, trigger cocked, to his head. One flick of that wicked finger, one false move on Aaron's part, and his life would be over. I couldn't explain how I knew that, but I did; and I was desperate to stop it.

Over the years I'd seen what the promises of God could do in my own life. I'd learned how to believe God's Word and, by believing, to release His miracle-working power in my body when I needed healing, for example, or in my finances when I was in need. But I'd never faced a situation like this. I'd never encountered such darkness when I prayed.

Some believers I knew suggested I just roll the care of the whole situation over on God and forget about it. That didn't seem right to me. If God wanted me to forget about Aaron, why had He given me such burden to pray for him? Why would He reveal to me the magnitude of the threat if I had no power to do anything about it?

Other well-meaning Christians suggested that, since my son was technically an adult now, he had to make his own choices and there was nothing I could do about it. "God won't override a person's will," they said. "Aaron is free to choose God or reject Him. You can pray all you want, but ultimately, what Aaron decides to do is up to him."

That sounded reasonable, even scriptural. Still, something within me rebelled against such theories. I listened to them politely on the outside, but inside my heart I raged in response. *Sure, that's easy for you to say! It's not your son we're talking about, it's mine! And I cannot bear to let the devil swallow him up. I cannot and I will not. God will show me a way to save him!*

After I slammed my ears shut to the naysayers around me, I was hounded by condemning voices in my own mind. Thoughts of my failures as a mother trailed after me. Yipping like a pack of dogs on a hunt, they tormented me with memories of my own backslidden past. The divorce that had left Aaron fatherless as a toddler, the years during his early childhood when I'd failed to take him to church, the busyness that blinded me to the seriousness of his situation in high school—all those things nipped at my heart, blaming me for what was happening to him now.

Thoughts of what I should have done differently or better gnawed away at me. *It's your fault. You made the mistakes. Now you'll have to live with them, and Aaron may die because of them. There's nothing you can do about it now.*

But there's something about a parent's love. All by itself, it is almost supernatural. Cut from the cloth of God's own compassion, a parent's love will never stop searching for a way to redeem its children. It will fight for them, if it must, to the death.

But sometimes, before love can win that fight, it must get mad.

That's what I did, early one morning as I knelt on the floor, poring over my Bible. Wrapped in a fuzzy bathrobe, staring sleepy-eyed at the scriptural promises for my children that I'd seen so many times, a flash of anger shot through me. "The devil has no right to Aaron!" I shouted, the full revelation of it surging through me at last. "I refuse to let this go on any longer. I will take these promises and pound the devil with them until he runs screaming out of my son's life because this is a battle the blood of Jesus has already won!"

Only once before in my life had I felt that kind of maternal fury. It was just a few weeks after Aaron was born. I had been wheeling him around the neighborhood for the first time in his stroller when I heard a low growl and turned to see a German shepherd lunging toward us with teeth bared and black lips foaming. To this day, I can't recall what on earth I was thinking. But the next thing I knew, I was shrieking a war whoop that rattled windows for blocks, hurtling toward that dog with fists clenched, ready to kill him before he laid a fang on my son.

Whether or not I actually could have done so is anybody's guess, but the dog decided to err on the side of caution. Tucking his tail between his hairy haunches, he spun 180 degrees in midair and bounded back into the suburban jungle from which he had come.

The encounter had taught him an important lesson: Don't mess with an angry mother—especially if she has a stroller in her hand.

Now, some nineteen years later, standing in an eerily similar situation, I felt that same anger again. Fueled by the promises I had found in God's Word, it erupted in a blast of spiritual fury that sent me hurtling toward my attacker with the vengeance of a warrior willing to die for her cause. My prayers grew fervent and fierce. The devil was about encounter a principle much like the one the German shepherd stumbled into: Don't mess with an angry mother—especially if she has a Bible in her hand.

Swinging the Sword of the Spirit

There are times in life when trouble comes and the Word of God is a comforting pillow that brings us rest. There are times when the Scriptures wrap around us like a blanket of God's wisdom and love. The Bible is a blessing when it serves us in that way.

But when we are fighting for someone's life, what we need is not the *pillow of the Spirit*, or the *blanket of the spirit*. What we need is the *sword of the spirit*, the weapon the apostle Paul referred to in Ephesians 6 where he wrote:

> *Finally, my brethren, be strong in the Lord and in the power of His might. Put on the whole armor of God, that you may be able to stand against the wiles of the devil. For we do not wrestle against flesh and blood, but against principalities, against powers, against the rulers of the darkness of this age, against spiritual hosts of wickedness in the heavenly places. Therefore take up the whole armor of God, that you may be able to withstand in the evil day, and having done all, to stand. Stand therefore, having girded your waist with truth, having put on the breastplate of righteousness, and having shod your feet with the preparation of the gospel of peace; above all, taking*

the shield of faith with which you will be able to quench all the fiery darts of the wicked one. And take the helmet of salvation, and the sword of the Spirit, which is the word of God; praying always with all prayer and supplication in the Spirit, being watchful to this end with all perseverance and supplication for all the saints. (verses 10–18)

It was the sword of the spirit that turned the prayer battle over Aaron in my favor. As I searched my Bible daily, the Holy Spirit lifted verses from the pages and placed them like gleaming spiritual daggers in my hand. He showed me that I am in Christ, and *"all the promises of God in Him are Yes, and in Him Amen"* (2 Corinthians 1:20); therefore the promises in the Old Testament belong as surely to me as those in the New. Among those Old Testament promises, I found one passage Isaiah that summed them all up for me. It says:

All your...children shall be disciples [taught by the Lord and obedient to His will], and great shall be the peace and undisturbed composure of your children...no weapon that is formed against you shall prosper, and ever tongue that shall rise against you in judgment you shall show to be in the wrong. This [peace, righteousness, security, triumph over opposition] is the heritage of the servants of the Lord.

(Isaiah 54:13, 17 AMP)

As far as I was concerned, those verses settled the issue. God had already declared His will for Aaron's future. He had written it in the pages of the Bible. God had destined in advance that, as the son of a believer, Aaron would be a follower of Jesus. God Himself had sworn in His written Word that He would personally teach my children, empower them to obey Him, and lead them into places of peace—spiritually and physically. Any weapon the devil formed against Aaron was doomed to fail because the Bible said so.

What's more, according to those verses, I need not cower under condemning accusations from my past. I could stand on the Word and triumph over them. I could throw off the blame the devil had heaped upon me and declare that Jesus shed His own blood to pay the price for all my sins, including the ones that had injured my children. I could call on His redemptive power to go to work on their behalf.

So that's exactly what I did. Day after day, I wrestled in prayer against the spiritual darkness that had enveloped my son. Refusing to give up until I could sense clearly in my heart that the battle had been won, I returned again and again to the throne room of grace, praying just as Paul told us to, with all kinds of prayer and supplication.

I had no real idea what kind of prayer would work best, so I just followed the leading of the Lord as it came to me. Sometimes I declared the Word. Other times I prayed militantly in the Holy Spirit. Occasionally I wept with groans and tears that erupted from the very core of my spirit. I'd never heard anyone else pray that way, but when I began to wonder if I'd lost my mind, the words of Romans 8:26–27 convinced me otherwise.

> So too the [Holy] Spirit comes to our aid and bears us up in our weakness; for we do not know what prayer to offer nor how to offer it worthily as we ought, but the Spirit Himself goes to meet our supplication and plead in our behalf with unspeakable yearnings and groanings too deep for utterance. And He Who searches the hearts of men knows what is in the mind of the [Holy] Spirit [what His intent is], because the Spirit intercedes and pleads [before God] in behalf of the saints according to and in harmony with God's will.   (AMP)

If the devil has any virtue at all, it would be this: he does not give up easily. I discovered this for myself as the days stretched into weeks and the weeks into months with no sign of change. Each time the phone rang, my heart lurched toward it as if to race my hand to the receiver and be the first to hear Aaron's voice again. But it was always someone else calling.

I carried him in my heart all the time but, of course, I couldn't spend all day on my knees. Life went on, and I had to go on with it: cooking meals for the family, meeting the relentless writing deadlines that marched toward me week after week, chauffeuring my daughter to and from school every day. During those months I learned what the Bible means when it says, *"Pray without ceasing"* (1 Thessalonians 5:17). I discovered that with the help of the Holy Spirit, I could keep my heart turned toward God in an attitude of faith even though my mind and body were occupied with other things.

When well-meaning friends or acquaintances called to talk to me about the situation—often to tell me they'd seen Aaron somewhere looking bedraggled and sporting a new tattoo—I refused to say anything about him except what the Bible said. I told them that, despite appearances to the contrary, God had given me His Word that Aaron is a disciple of the Lord and I had no doubt that Word would prevail. I realized I sounded like I was in denial, but I didn't care what others thought. Their opinions wouldn't save my son; faith in God's Word would, so I chose to stick with faith.

To everyone else, it appeared that all my hours of praying, all my standing against the devil and declaring the Word had made not one whit of difference. But appearances can be deceiving, and I knew in my heart God was on the move.

How Will You Reach Him?

Hundreds of miles away in Edmond, Aaron's circumstances began to change. Early one morning after partying all night, he stumbled back to his gangster friend's apartment and found the locks changed. A note on the door read, *Look in the storage closet.* There, Aaron found his clothes and other belongings stuffed in garbage bags and ready to move.

With no money and no friends left who would put up with him, he was homeless.

The only thing he knew to do was call his older brother, Christopher, who in years past had been one of his best friends and strongest spiritual allies. Christopher was living in a house nearby with a couple of friends from church. Maybe they would help. It was worth a try.

Aaron found a pay phone and dialed the number.

Christopher watched, amazed, as Aaron lugged his garbage bag suitcases into the spare bedroom. He and Aaron had grown up together, sung in church musicals together, even prayed together. But looking at Aaron now, he didn't even know him. Every trace of spiritual light had disappeared from his eyes. Everything about him was cold, hard, and hopeless.

The friends Christopher shared a house with had agreed to let Aaron move in and live rent-free for a while until he got on his feet. Since they'd all gone to church together years before, they'd known Aaron as he used to be. They figured, surely, with his life in such a shambles, Aaron would quickly turn back to the Lord.

To their dismay, he didn't. Instead, he spent the nights he wasn't playing gigs or partying slumped on the sofa, staring at the floor, and picking his guitar to the strains of Nirvana.

Christopher hated to admit it, but it almost seemed as if God Himself had given up on Aaron, as if the Holy Spirit, too grieved to linger any longer in his hardened heart had turned out the lights and departed. From all appearances, the door was locked and the place was empty. There was no longer anyone home.

Too kind to further bruise my hopeful heart by telling me how bad Aaron looked, when Christopher called to give me an update, all he told me was that his brother had moved in.

Even if Christopher had shared the disheartening details, they wouldn't have discouraged me; by that time I was living in an alternate reality. All I could see was what God's Word said about Aaron. No matter how spiritually hollow he might appear, I knew God would never abandon him. I had His Word on it as surely as if the Holy Spirit had inscribed on my heart with some heavenly pen God's personal promise:

> "As for Me," says the LORD, "this is My covenant...My Spirit who is upon you, and My words which I have put in your mouth, shall not depart from your mouth, nor from the mouth of your descendants, nor from the mouth of your descendants' descendants," says the LORD, "from this time and forevermore."
>
> (Isaiah 59:21)

I had no doubt God intended to keep that promise. There was just one problem. Time had run out. The devil was no longer just stalking Aaron; he was moving in for the kill.

Driving home one morning from my daughter's school, an unexplainable urgency enveloped me. For no apparent reason, my heart galloped out of control and my hands trembled on the wheel. *Aaron!* I could feel someone calling his name. The sound of it came from within me.

Scrambling for an explanation, I flashed back fifteen years to another moment I'd heard Aaron's name just the same way. He and Christopher, both just chubby-cheeked boys at the time, had been playing together in a park near our home in west Texas. My view of them had been blocked by a scraggly crowd of Mesquite trees as I batted tennis balls around a cracked cement court with my husband on the other side of the park.

I'd always assumed it was Christopher who sounded the alarm. *Aaron!* The cry didn't pierce the air and grab my attention as such cries usually do. Instead, it seeped into my consciousness from the inside out. *Aaron!* When the call finally registered, my husband and I threw down our tennis rackets and raced toward the boys.

When we reached them, we found four-year-old Aaron floundering, blue-faced and breathless, in a drainage ditch filled with water. Christopher, unwilling to leave him but unable to save him, stood sobbing in panic nearby. I'd known the minute we saw Aaron's face blurred and contorted beneath the ripples he made as he thrashed for his life, how close to death he'd come. Had we ignored the warning cry, or delayed in answering, Aaron would have been a tragic memory.

It wasn't until years later when our family was reminiscing about the event that we all learned the truth. Christopher, frozen with fear, had not even thought to cry out that day. He had never made a sound.

His claim confounded us. "Who was it, then, that called us?" I asked.

"There was a man there," said Christopher. "He told me he would go get you and he did."

But neither my husband nor I had seen any man that day. There were no other people in that dusty west Texas park. We were sure of it. Someone else, some divine messenger sent to help protect the children of the righteous, had sounded the alarm.

Now it was happening again. *Aaron!* I considered pulling to the side of the road and praying in my car but decided to pray while I drove instead. As I did, the tension mounted within me, pulling my heart as taut as an archer's bow. At home, I burst through the door and crumpled to my knees on the living room floor. Weeping, praying in the Spirit, claiming God's promises—I released the arrows of my faith and sent soaring toward them mark. Then, all at once, I fell silent.

A peace unlike anything I'd experienced in the previous months flooded not just my heart but the whole room. The battle was over. We had won. I was almost certain. Only one question remained in my mind, so I asked it.

"Lord, how will You reach him? He has cut himself off from every godly influence."

I will never forget the answer that came.

I will reach him even if I have to go Myself.

Coming Home

From then on, all I could do was rejoice. Although I heard nothing from Aaron for weeks afterward, I found it impossible to be concerned about him. I knew my prayers had been answered.

One July day, the phone rang. When I answered, I heard the voice of my beloved prodigal, choking with tears.

"Mom? It's Aaron," he said. "Can I come home?"

I listened in amazement as he told me what had happened. Two nights earlier he had been in bed—whether he was asleep or awake he couldn't say for sure—when a vision as clear as any movie unfolded before his eyes. In the vision, a man driving a black car had aimed a gun at Aaron's head and fired.

I don't know what it's like to watch myself die, but my son does because he has done it. Terrified but unable to move, he watched his life snuffed out. He saw his own end, and it was horrible, miserable, and stupid.

He would have fled at the sight but a divine force held him to his bed. Pinned like a wrestler to the mat by Someone infinitely stronger than he, Aaron finally heard and listened to the God he had been running from. *"If you do not repent, you will be dead before the year is out,"* He said. *"And this is the way you will die."*

Scared sober but unsure of what to do, Aaron spent the next day pondering his situation. When night fell, he found himself listening to an old rock song about a father's love. It was then that the Lord spoke to him again and gave him the instructions he needed. "Call your mother. It's time to go home."

Many years later as he was telling me again how it all happened, I shared with him what the Lord had promised. "He said that He would reach you, even if He had to go Himself."

Aaron smiled and nodded, rehearsing the memory of those nights in his mind. "Yes...I suppose you could say that's exactly what He did."

When the Bomb Goes Off

The spoils of righteous war are always worth the fight. That's especially true when the battle is over your children. It's a matter of honor with God to ensure that everything the devil steals is restored sevenfold to those who will stand to the end. So it's no wonder the joy I felt over the next few months defies description.

By September, Aaron was not only back home, he was attending Bible college and working part-time at an international Christian ministry. He dove into the activities at the church we attended—a congregation aptly named Happy Church, pastored by Wally and Marilyn Hickey. As if in recompense for the rejection Aaron had experienced years earlier, the youth pastor there, a firebrand named Mike Donahue, swept Aaron under his wing and put him to work teaching high school Bible study groups and leading worship in the youth services. Mike wasn't critical of Aaron's past. He'd come through some rough times himself. He knew what God had done in his own life and he trusted Him to do the same in Aaron's.

Just when I thought things couldn't get any better, Aaron told me Mike had paired the home Bible study leaders up in teams. Aaron's co-leader happened to be a beautiful, young blonde named Krista Thompson.

Okay, Lord, I smiled, *now, You're just showing off.*

I'd first seen Krista a year earlier asking eager questions at a morning Bible seminar class I'd attended at the church. When I saw her, I had prayed a blatantly selfish prayer. "Father, that's the kind of girl I want Aaron to marry someday."

Of course, all that was many years ago now. These days, Aaron and Krista are no longer leading youth Bible studies together. They're raising my grandkids and pastoring the church they planted a few years ago, Lifesong Worship Center.

The devil failed to disarm the time spiritual bomb that was ticking in my once-troubled son. Just as he feared, it exploded and hurled Aaron into a life of ministry that has done significant damage to the kingdom of darkness. Through his years working as a youth pastor and worship leader, souls have been won to Jesus, believers have been discipled, and thousands of people have found their way through worship into the presence of the Lord.

If I ever start to take those things for granted, I think back to the time years ago when Aaron spent his nights performing in bars with a rock band instead of leading worship on Sundays. I never met any of the other four young men in that band, and I guess I never will. Three of them are already dead: one committed suicide, one died in a car accident, one overdosed.

If the devil had gotten his way, Aaron's name would have been added to that list; but God had a different plan. He promised me that all my children would be His disciples, taught by Him and obedient to His Word. He gave me His Word that they would live in peace. That's a promise He has kept.

More Enemies to Conquer

If I ever entertained the idea that once Aaron was back in the fold, I could take a vacation from praying for the children of the saints—my own or anyone else's—I quickly let it go. God did not intend for me to take the scriptural promises I discovered and hang them on the wall as trophies of past victories. There were other enemies to conquer.

Additional battles had to be fought for my own children, of course, because the devil never just gives up and goes home; but most of those skirmishes were brief and easily won. It's not that the devil's plots grew less sinister, it's just that during those two long years praying for Aaron, I'd learned some crucial lessons and become more skilled in spiritual warfare. That's the risk the devil always runs. If he attacks and by the grace of God we lay hold of the wisdom and spiritual strength to defeat him, he has not only lost a battle, he has gained a more dangerous foe.

No one understands that better than the Lord Jesus Himself, who is the acting Commander of all of heaven's armies. As the Lord of Hosts, He knows the strengths and weaknesses of His earthly forces. He knows what weapons they've learned to wield and where those weapons are needed at any given moment. So we should never be surprised, once we've personally gained victory in a certain area, to find ourselves fighting shoulder-to-shoulder with fellow believers who are struggling to take that same ground themselves.

Ten years after the war over Aaron had been won, God called me into action again on a bone-chilling Wednesday night in the middle of New York snowstorm. To say I answered His call cheerfully would be an exaggeration. I tried to convince myself I should cancel the prayer meeting I was scheduled to lead at the church that night. *Surely,* I reasoned, *that's what God in His great mercy would want me to do.* He knew even better than I that the snow was piling up faster than the road crews could clear it; and even after the snowplows grumbled by and scraped the streets clean, the winds sheared the tops off the snowdrifts on the roadside and undid the job.

"This is crazy…absolutely crazy," I muttered as I coasted the Jeep into the church parking lot. "The place looks like Siberia, for Pete's sake! Nobody's going to show up for prayer tonight."

Sure enough, only three snow-encrusted pray-ers straggled in, shaking out their coats and wool scarves as they came. Among them was Jackie. *I should have known.* Jackie hadn't missed a prayer meeting in who knows how many years. She'd been praying heaven and earth together for the people of this church for longer than the devil cared to remember.

But, despite the spiritual victories she'd won for others, Jackie carried her own private grief. Her college-age son had never been saved. He lived in another city, so I'd never met him, but from the bits and pieces she'd had said about him, I gathered that much like Aaron, he'd been through some tough experiences that had hardened his heart toward the Lord. I figured if Jackie's prayers hadn't softened him in all these years, he must be one crusty character.

Honestly, I didn't intend to pray for him that night. But the Holy Spirit surprised us by sweeping us into intercession for him. As I bowed on the sanctuary steps praying beside his desperate mother, all the faith God had developed in me through my battle over Aaron sprang back to life.

I don't remember all we prayed that night. I just know that Jackie and I drew our spiritual swords together, declaring one scriptural promise after another, until we actually felt the forces of darkness turn tail and run. *"Resist the devil and he will flee from you"* is what James 4:7 says, and that night we proved it's true.

One thing I do remember. We ended our prayer with this victorious proclamation on our lips: *"And it shall come to pass in the last days, says God, that I will pour out of My Spirit on all flesh; Your sons and your daughters shall prophesy"* (Acts 2:17). With that declaration, the same peace I'd experienced years earlier when praying for my own son flooded the place. When it did, Jackie and I knew her boy's salvation had been won. Together we had activated the promise of Jesus: *"If two of you shall agree on earth as touching any thing that they shall ask, it shall be done for them by my Father in heaven"* (Matthew 18:19).

Sometime before dawn the next morning, the telephone on Jackie's bedside table rang, jarring her awake. When she answered, she heard the words she'd been waiting for years to hear.

"Mom? I need you to pray with me. I can't stand my life anymore. I want to confess my sins and get saved tonight."

Not Just for Prodigals

Over the years, I have seen that kind of thing happen again and again. I've seen parents whose kids were caught in the most demonic traps imaginable grab hold of God's promises, refuse to let go, and see miracles in their children's lives.

I remember one mother who first heard about God's promises for our children when her son was locked up in the city jail—the product of a broken home, an impoverished background, and a violent inner-city neighborhood. But she dared to believe God was mightier than all those things. She stood on the Scriptures and began to pray. Within six months, her son was a whole new man.

He'd dedicated his life to the Lord, left his jailhouse days behind, and enrolled in college.

God's promises aren't just reserved for prodigals, either. The same promise that will bring home a wayward son will heal, deliver, and protect our children in times of danger. It will open barren wombs and bring forth the sons and daughters the devil has tried to deny us.

The Bible leaves no doubt about it. Nothing is more precious to God than the children of His people. They are included in almost every scriptural promise He gives us. The stories that follow bear that out again and again. Each one proves in its own unique way that God meant it when He said, *"All your children shall be taught by the* LORD, *and great shall be the peace of your children"* (Isaiah 54:13).

Part Two

A GOD WHO KEEPS HIS PROMISES

By Melanie

Part Two

A GOD WHO KEEPS HIS PROMISES

Broken Heart

Thousands of tiny flames flickered across the dark horizon as 600,000 fans lifted their lighters aloft and swayed to the rhythm of Mylon Le Fevre's music. They watched, mesmerized, as Mylon's hair whipped across his sweat-dampened face, the dark strands dancing to the frenzied beat that pounded from his heart, coursed through his veins, and pulsed through every cell of his being. One with the notes and one with his audience, Mylon had never felt more alive.

Onstage he was bigger than life, a hero to his adoring fans. Looking out at the sea of starstruck faces, a wave of gratitude swept over him. This was a moment he'd never imagined when he began singing gospel music with his family at the tender age of twelve.

Who could have guessed back then that a poor boy from Georgia would end up here in Paris, France, at an international pop festival performing with some of the most famous musicians in the world?

For a kid who'd once been barred from the school choir, standing on this stage and listening to the thunderous applause of more than a half million people was sweet revenge. Life didn't get much better than this.

If only he could stay onstage forever. But, he couldn't; so when the last note faded and the crowd streamed onto the streets of Paris, Mylon ducked into the back seat of his waiting limo.

Resting his head against the tinted window, he scanned the skyline for the *Arc de Triomphe* as the driver threaded his way through the Paris streets to the opulent King George V Hotel. There, in a luxury suite only steps from the *Champs-Élysées*, Mylon would spend his nights as he always did, sharing his fame and success with his two constant companions: loneliness and a gnawing emotional pain that never went away.

Sighing, he knew he'd have to take something to curtail the cocaine rush that kept his heart hammering away like a drummer on steroids. No amount of money, not even the shimmering streets of Paris, could glamorize snorting cocaine and heroin. But it was the only thing he knew that would soothe the monster within and let him sleep.

The French drugs were more pure, uncut, and powerful than those Mylon bought back in the United States. A few nights later, unaware of the danger, he didn't reduce his dose. As the minutes ticked by, he realized his mistake. He choked like he'd swallowed a bale of cotton as his fingernails and lips turned blue. Suffocating, he lost consciousness again and again.

Through his drug-induced stupor, twenty-seven-year-old Mylon Le Fevre knew one thing with crystal clarity. He had overdosed and he was dying. He'd lived like hell and never expected to survive past age thirty. About to meet his maker, Mylon struggled to recall the God of his youth, the One he'd sung to as a boy. He couldn't pray, not after the way he'd lived. But he knew someone who could.

Fumbling for the telephone beside his bed, Mylon mumbled a request to the operator who connected him long distance to the last person he figured he'd ever talk to this side of eternity. "Mama," he said, his speech slurred and his eyes misty, "pray for me."

Eva Mae Le Fevre knew her youngest son had lived like the devil, but the devil wasn't going to win the war for this prodigal if she could help it. She prayed like Mylon's life depended on it. Comforted by the sound, just as the sun dawned on a new day, Mylon Le Fevre's world faded to black.

Jesus Jazz

It wasn't a fitting end for the son of the famous gospel singing family, The Le Fevres. Young Mylon hadn't been raised in a world of drugs and death. He'd grown up surrounded by songs about Jesus and eternal life. By the time he learned to walk, he was toddling around listening to rehearsals, his quick mind and hungry heart memorizing notes while watching nimble fingers play all the instruments. As soon as he could stretch his own small hand around the fret, he'd learned to play the ukulele, the mandolin, the guitar, and the bass. By the time he was twelve years old, Mylon sang with the family and made his first recording.

He'd started his life with dreams of making music for the Lord, singing with his family for years to come. While being a part of the famous Le Fevres had its advantages, it also had its drawbacks. With his parents' concert schedule, they were away most of the time. His mother wasn't there to help him with homework after school. His father wasn't around to pitch a ball or teach him how to deal with bullies. Shuffled from one school to another, Mylon attended eleven different schools in twelve years.

During his freshman year in high school, Mylon lived in Greenville, South Carolina, and attended the academy at Bob Jones University. Homesick for his family, he clung with tenacity to the music they had inspired within him. At school, he played the piano and sang to audition for a class in voice. "Your music is totally unacceptable," he was told. "You're dismissed!"

They wouldn't even let him sing in the choir. Feeling rejected and alone, Mylon played his parents' records just to hear his mother's voice.

"That's *Jesus jazz!*" school officials said about his parents' southern gospel music. When they confiscated all of his parents' music, forbidding him to listen to it and condemning them for singing it, anger simmered beneath his calm exterior. The beast that would one day control him had raised its ugly head.

Mylon hadn't seen his family in months when his parents called and told him they would be singing at a concert in Greenville. Breathless with excitement, Mylon announced that he would see his parents soon. But school authorities refused to allow him even to attend the concert. When his father, furious over the school's decision, picked Mylon up and took him anyway, Mylon was expelled from school.

The decision was so unfair that Mylon's anger grew from a simmer to a slow boil. The seed of rage against religion and legalism was planted deep in his heart.

Song of the Lord

By the time he was a senior, Mylon attended the academy at the West Coast Bible College in Fresno, California. At age seventeen, he'd attained a measure of peace and was pursuing God with all of his heart. He sang in the school choir, attended chapel every morning, studied his Bible, and prayed. None of the rejection he suffered had been powerful enough to stop the music and lyrics that bubbled up from his heart each day. It didn't stop the instruments he heard within him.

Sitting on his bunk one morning, Mylon read John 15:5, "I am the vine, you are the branches. He who abides in Me, and I in him, bears much fruit; for without Me you can do nothing." *Without Him I could do nothing!* The revelation sparked a melody and Mylon penned the words to his newest song, "Without Him."

Small for his age, Mylon stood five feet four inches tall and weighed a mere 120 pounds. School bullies enjoyed tormenting him, and the jocks considered Mylon a sissy who wrote poems—their definition of his lyrics. Fighting to defend himself, Mylon was labeled a rebel. Once again he was expelled in shame over a minor offense.

He moved back to Georgia, got a job, rented a room in a boarding house and finished high school on his own. Soon afterward he enlisted in the army. Over the next six months Mylon grew seven inches taller and gained thirty-five pounds. In 1962, while Mylon was stationed at Fort Jackson, South Carolina, his parents called. "We're going to sing at the Gospel Quartet Convention in Memphis," his mother said. "If you can get there I'd like you to sing 'Without Him.'"

Snagging a weekend pass, Mylon hitchhiked more than six hundred miles to Memphis. Onstage with his parents, Mylon had no way of knowing that in a private room in the convention center, the biggest star in the world watched and listened behind mirrored glass. Afterward, Elvis Presley asked to meet him. Elvis recorded "Without Him," making it a hit. Within a year, 126 other artists—including Johnny Cash—had also recorded the song.

After his discharge from the military, Mylon joined the Stamps Quartet. Music and lyrics bubbled up in him so fast that Mylon wrote songs like some people wrote their diary. Less than two years later, Mylon's father wooed him back to the Le Fevres. "You're a Le Fevre," his dad said. "You belong with us."

By age twenty-five, Mylon was married and owned his own home. He wrote, published, arranged, produced, and performed songs with The Le Fevres. Then his father fired him because his sideburns were a half-inch too long.

"I'm a grown man," Mylon protested. "I should be able to wear my sideburns the way I want."

"Not in my group," his father said, his jaw set.

A New Sound

Heartsick with rejection, Mylon felt unable to find his place in the family. His father wanted Mylon to be like him: play bass with his thumb instead of his fingers; hold the bass guitar higher instead of lower; sing southern gospel instead of Christian rock; admire Frank Sinatra instead of The Beatles. His dad had formed the first Christian recording company and the first syndicated television show. A pioneer in his own time, he believed that the new sound of rock and roll and Christian rock were no more than passing fads.

Father and son were separated by a generation gap wider than the Grand Canyon.

That would have been bad enough, but many Christians didn't approve of an upbeat rocking tempo even if the lyrics gave praise and glory to God. Rejected by family and by much of organized religion, Mylon felt frustrated with his inability to find his place in his family and the family of faith.

At age twenty-five, Mylon started his own band with three of the people who would later form the Atlanta Rhythm Section. As his fame grew, George Harrison of The Beatles, Ron Wood from the Rolling Stones, Mick Fleetwood from Fleetwood Mac, Eric Clapton, Alvin Lee from Ten Years After, Steve Winwood, Billy Joel, Elton John, Tina Turner, Little Richard, and others all sang or played on Mylon's records. Mylon also sang and recorded with The Who.

Although Mylon never recorded an album that didn't include songs that gave glory to God, inside the pain of rejection gnawed at him. He anesthetized it with marijuana…then with cocaine…and finally with heroin. When heroin wrapped its sinewy claws around him, Mylon's addiction left him incapable of having a relationship with God. Heroin was his mistress, a fickle lover whose dirge of death was destroying his life.

Ashamed and brokenhearted, Mylon lost the confidence to pray. The journey from the joyful innocence that inspired "Without Him" to a heroin overdose in Paris had been long and painful. Phone in hand, listening to his mother's prayer, he left his misery behind and drifted into unconsciousness.

Living without Him

The next afternoon, Mylon awoke not in heaven or hell, but in the same plush suite at the King George V. He blinked, his eyes unfocused. *I'm alive.* How in the world had that happened? He didn't know whether to laugh for joy or weep in despair. Had God saved him for a purpose? Or had his mother's prayer just bought him a little time?

His body screaming for drugs, Mylon stumbled out of bed and found his stash. As the chemicals coursed through his veins, he could almost hear his mother praying again. Mylon knew his mother would never stop praying for him.

It was a good thing; only God could help him now.

Mylon picked up his life where he'd left off before the overdose. He moved to England to resume his rock star lifestyle (beyond the reach of the American police who had arrested him for drug possession too many times) and in 1973 began recording a new album entitled "On the Road to Freedom." Even Mylon's chemically addled brain couldn't miss the irony of singing about freedom while on the road to certain death, trapped in a prison of addiction and despair.

Curtain Call

Laughter mixed with excited chatter rose above the music that rocked through the stereo. Shot glasses clinked in celebration of the biggest rock tour of Mylon's career. Alcohol and drugs flowed like Niagara Falls. With the party in full swing no one noticed Mylon's absence.

One of the guests paused mid-sentence and wrinkled her nose. "What's that awful smell?"

Someone else put down his drink and furrowed his brow. "Is something burning?" Following the scent, the man went to investigate. The color drained from his face at the sight before him. Thirty-year-old Mylon Le Fevre had overdosed again. Lips purple and eyes fixed, he had stopped breathing. The cigarette between his fingers had burned away his flesh. Paramedics worked in a fevered pitch on Mylon's lifeless body as the ambulance screamed to the hospital.

Mylon Le Fevre wasn't the same man or the same artist when he woke from the coma. No one knew how long he'd been without oxygen when he quit breathing, but it had been long enough to cause brain damage. He couldn't even remember the lyrics to his own songs.

A broken shell of a man, Mylon's career was finished. He was depressed and addicted. Life as he knew it was over. Like the prodigal son in the Bible, he'd wasted his life in sin and could only dream of his Father's house.

The Long Road Home

Mylon pulled a Gideon Bible from the bedside table in his hospital room and read the words that had comforted him as a boy, *"For God so loved the world that He gave His only begotten Son, that whoever believes in Him should not perish but have everlasting life"* (John 3:16). God *loved*. Mylon ached for that love. He yearned to fall into his Father's arms...but he couldn't. Trapped by feelings of unworthiness, Mylon struggled for several years to forgive himself, but he couldn't find his way back home.

In 1974, God sent someone to help him.

Two members of Andre Crouch's backup band took a strung-out Mylon with them to Jack Hayford's church. Outside after church, someone said, "Aren't you Mylon Le Fevre?"

Mylon turned, half-recognizing the familiar voice. Now that he was back in the States, he wasn't used to bumping into people he knew.

"I'm Buck Herring, and I love your 'We Believe' album."

Buck Herring? Mylon smiled, glad to bump into another Christian musician, an acquaintance from the past who had engineered "I Am Woman" for Helen Reddy.

Over the next six years, Buck Herring ministered the love of God to Mylon. Only one thing stood between Mylon and getting right with God: heroin, a faithless mistress who had wound him in such a web of bondage that he despaired of ever getting free.

In 1980, Buck Herring phoned Mylon in Atlanta. "Mylon," Buck said, "my wife and I are going to be in Atlanta doing a concert with our band, 2nd Chapter of Acts. I'd love for you to come."

During the concert, Mylon felt as though he had stepped into an alternate reality. The performers had long hair. They weren't concerned about outward appearances; they were concerned with issues of the heart. The music—beautiful and alive—swirled around him like rivers of peace. The 2nd Chapter of Acts didn't sing about Jesus; they sang *to* Him.

The presence of God was so palpable that Mylon wept before the Lord. Never in his life—not in any church—had he stepped into the presence of God in such a profound way.

I made Jesus my savior years ago, Mylon realized. *But I have to make Him Lord of everything in my life. I can't get free without Him. Jesus must be the Lord even of my addiction to heroin.* There, in the middle of a concert, Mylon Le Fevre rushed headlong into his Father's arms. Walking out of the auditorium that night, he realized that his life would never be the same.

Healing the Brokenhearted

Jesus not only healed Mylon's broken heart, he delivered him from the bondage of drug addiction. Mylon went back to his home church in Atlanta and accepted a job cleaning the toilets. For Mylon, cleaning toilets in the kingdom of God was a promotion over limousines and Lear jets, living in castles and penthouses on his way to hell. Ravenous for God, he attended five Bible studies a week.

Within months God gave Mylon a new song, "Brand New Start," which Mylon sang in prison, offering hope to other brokenhearted men. Soon, God assembled members of a new band, Mylon and Broken Heart.

"We're called to go back to the gutter that God saved us from," Mylon told his band. "We're going to play in jails, prisons, and to junkies in rehab." Eventually the Lord opened doors for them to perform in coliseums, arenas, and stadiums.

"If God can deliver me," Mylon said after giving his testimony at each concert, "He can deliver anyone." Over the next ten years, Mylon and his band, Broken Heart, led more than 200,000 young people to Jesus.

When Mylon Le Fevre returned home to his Father's house, God treated him just like the prodigal son in the Bible. He dressed him in fine robes and put His signet ring on his finger. Restored to his place in God's family, Mylon released eleven new albums, received a Grammy award and two Dove awards, and sold millions of records. Eventually, he passed on his anointing for music to his son-in-law whose band, the Newsboys, rock and roll the truth about Jesus into the hearts of countless young people much like Mylon's band, Broken Heart, once did.

God didn't do a partial work in restoring to Mylon all that the enemy had stolen from him. He healed his body from the effects of years of drug use. God also brought him a beautiful and godly wife, Christi, who is an outstanding author and teacher.

Today, Mylon and Christi travel the world spreading the good news that God has thrown open the door to His house.

He's calling the prodigals home.

He's healing their broken hearts.

Fairy Tale Faith

The sultry evening air hung as heavy as the Spanish moss that draped the oak trees, too tired to stir in the brutal heat. Kellie

Domby stepped outside her Alabama home and felt as though she'd walked into a steam bath, the cloying sweet-sick air too thick to breathe. Katydids buzzed in nearby trees, as certain a sign of summer as the temperatures that hovered in triple digits. In the sixth month of Kellie's pregnancy, only the doctor's admonition to walk stirred her from the cool air inside.

Brad, Kellie's husband, stepped outside to join her and felt a furnace blast of heat assault him. They strolled, too hot to hurry, and enjoyed a companionable silence. Kellie had always prayed for a fairy tale romance, and theirs had been just that. While in college, Kellie's best friend's family had been stationed in Germany. In Spain for a semester of study, Kellie flew to Germany to spend Christmas with her friend. Snowflakes had floated on the cold, crisp air on Christmas Eve when Kellie walked downstairs and saw Brad Domby.

I love him! Kellie thought, pausing on the stairs as her face flushed the color of her bright pink sweater. Although she'd never laid eyes on him before that moment, Kellie knew with settled certainty that this man was her mate. After a magical week talking and sightseeing, Brad went back to the base where he was stationed in the Germany and Kellie flew home to Michigan.

The following August, back in Germany, Brad had taken Kellie to visit the Neuschwanstein Castle; the one Disney copied for *Sleeping Beauty*. There against the backdrop of the Bavarian Alps, Brad Domby knelt and proposed. Less than a year after their fairy tale romance began, Brad and Kellie were married. Now, six happy years later, they were expecting their first child.

Life doesn't get any better than this, Kellie thought as they arrived home after their walk. Brad was already asleep when Kellie felt cramps sear across her abdomen. She woke Brad, who reassured her. "You probably just overdid it on the walk," he said.

Less than an hour later, she woke him again.

"It's worse," she said.

"Why don't you call the hospital and talk to a labor and delivery nurse?" Brad suggested. Kellie made the call and felt calmed by the experienced nurse's suggestion.

"You may be dehydrated," the nurse explained. "Drink four cups of water, and if the cramps continue, call me back."

Kellie drank the water, but the cramps intensified, coming five to eight minutes apart; then she began to bleed.

"I'm bleeding!" Kellie told Brad. They prayed on the way to the nearest Army hospital.

"We don't have a neonatal unit here," the Army doctor explained before sending Kellie by ambulance to a regional hospital. Fighting fear, Kellie felt relieved when a whole team of doctors met her in labor and delivery. A machine monitored her contractions while magnesium injected into her thigh finally stopped them.

"We'll keep you here for a few days until we can wean you off the magnesium," the doctor explained. "But you're going to have to stay in bed for the rest of your pregnancy."

That night, Kellie lay in her darkened hospital room with wide eyes. It was July and she wasn't due until October! Since his promotion to major, Brad's job required long hours. Their family lived far away, and they'd just relocated from New Jersey to Alabama and still didn't know anyone. How could she stay in bed for four months without help? She didn't know, but she'd do *anything* to keep her baby alive.

A few days later, Kellie was moved from labor and delivery to a regular floor. Off the magnesium injections, she received an oral medication to stop the contractions. By mid-afternoon she suffered mild cramps. The nurse notified the intern on call.

"The monitor isn't registering them as contractions," he said, dismissing the problem. By seven p.m. Kellie's pains were eight minutes apart and regular. The nurse couldn't find the intern. No one examined her.

"You're just tired," a nurse explained around midnight when Kellie complained again. The nurse gave her a sleeping pill.

An hour later, the nurse from labor and delivery checked on Kellie and decided to move her back there.

"She's bulging!" the nurse screamed when she examined Kellie. "Get a doctor in here *now!*"

Too Little...Too Soon

Before a doctor arrived, the nurse delivered a tiny, premature boy who was whisked away to the neonatal intensive care unit. Weighing in at two pounds, seven and a half ounces, David Domby was put on a ventilator, connected to a cardiac monitor, and nourished through an IV and a feeding tube.

Two of the babies—both larger than David—died. "Don't look around you," Brad instructed Kellie. "We've got to follow God, and that means keeping our eyes on Him and speaking His Word."

If watching other babies die took a toll on Kellie, it was nothing compared to listening to the doctors recite the dismal chances of David's survival. "If he *does* survive," the doctor continued, "he could be deaf, retarded, suffer a terminal illness...."

"*No!*" Kellie commanded. "That's enough! None of those things will happen to my son!"

While Brad had been raised in a church where he learned the power of God's Word, and the importance of believing and speaking it, Kellie had not. But for a time, Kellie had worked in the editorial department of a major ministry. She read the letters written by people whose lives had been forever changed by the power of God. She worked on articles about everyday people—not super saints—who dared to take God at His word. In almost every instance, there was a battle, but the end result had been miraculous.

Kellie Domby's fairy tale life crumpled before her eyes. Somebody was trying to kill her child, and she knew without a doubt that it wasn't God. She realized that what she and Brad believed in their hearts and spoke with their mouths from this moment on would make the difference between life and death for their child.

Little David's silken halo of surfer-blonde hair glistened in the incubator lights as he fought for his life. Standing beside him, Brad spoke words straight out of the Bible over his son. "With long life God will satisfy you, David, and show you His salvation."

"You are strong in God," Kellie added, "and in the power of His might."

"That's right," Brad agreed, "although you are small today, your faith makes you strong."

A few days later, Kellie was discharged from the hospital. "Most premature infants have to stay in the hospital at *least* until their due date," the medical staff explained. "David won't be discharged before October."

Kellie pushed her hand through the incubator opening and David grabbed her finger. "He'll leave early," Kellie said, feeling her son's tiny hand search out her own.

Every day Brad and Kellie spoke God's Word over their son. They made each negative report from the medical staff a matter of prayer. While several babies in the neonatal unit had been on ventilators for months, Brad and Kellie prayed, and David was taken off the ventilator in only two days.

When doctor's explained that David might require heart surgery to close a hole in his heart common in premature infants, Brad and Kellie prayed that it would close on its own.

It did.

After David received three blood transfusions, Brad and Kellie learned it wasn't unusual for some preemies to have eight or more transfusions before their blood cells worked properly. They spoke daily that David's blood cells were whole.

He didn't require any more transfusions.

On September 5, almost a month before he had been due, David Domby was discharged from the hospital. In preparation, the doctor required Brad and Kellie to learn infant CPR. David went home with a strap around his chest and a monitor that would alarm if he quit breathing.

"You can take it off when you're feeding him," the doctor explained, "because you'll be able to see if he stops breathing. David is suffering from gastric reflux and if stomach contents come up and block his lungs it could be fatal."

The Darkest Hour

Four days later, on September 9, an exhausted Kellie rose at two a.m. to feed the baby. As usual, the act of breathing and eating exhausted David and he drifted off to sleep. Only this time he didn't wake up.

Blinking bleary eyes, Kellie watched David's chest for movement.

There was none.

"Brad, I don't think David's breathing!" she cried.

Jumping out of bed, Brad ran to his son. "He's not! Call 911!" Brad said, starting CPR.

Kellie called 911 and then dialed Brad's mother, a powerful intercessor and prayer warrior. "Please pray!" she said. "David's not breathing!"

She watched Brad puff air into the baby's lungs, but his chest didn't rise. Stomach contents must have blocked his lungs!

Brad turned him over and performed the baby Heimlich to clear his airway. "Watch and see if his chest rises now," Brad ordered.

"It's still not moving!" Kellie cried.

Brad tried the Heimlich maneuver again. "Come on, Baby! Come on, Son!" Back to CPR, David's tiny chest still did not move.

It's been ten minutes and he still hasn't had any oxygen! Kellie thought, walking around the room and praying for her son. By now David's body was purple.

In one horrifying moment, the lifeless body expelled all its fluids.

In agony, Brad refused to stop trying to resuscitate his son.

Pacing and praying, Kellie's mind flashed back to a women's retreat she'd attended. "When you pray," the speaker had said, "see the situation resolved."

Kellie's mind raced back to her training as an altar minister. "When you pray for someone, see the result! See the blind eyes opened! See the dead raised to life!"

Closing her eyes, Kellie pictured David alive, happy, and joyful. She saw him running and playing. "David will live and not die!" she declared.

Across the country, the Holy Spirit revealed to Brad's mother that the baby had died. "I command life back into his body!" she decreed with authority.

Back home in Alabama, an emergency medical technician burst into the room. "Here, give him to me," he ordered, grabbing David's lifeless body.

At that moment, the power of God shot like lightening from the throne room of heaven into David Domby's corpse. Before the man could initiate any rescue efforts, David's chest rose in a long shuddering breath.

An ambulance screamed its way to the hospital with its precious cargo. When they arrived, Brad and Kellie heard a sound that made them weep for joy.

David cried.

Back on oxygen, connected to wires and monitors, David drank in air as he cried with indignation. "Gastric reflux caused stomach contents to cut off his breathing," the doctor explained. "He's alive, but he will most likely have pneumonia from aspirating stomach contents into his lungs. In addition, after going so long without oxygen, he could have brain damage."

Kellie Domby just smiled, unmoved by the doctor's words.

She and Brad stepped into the hall to talk. "Are you okay?" Brad asked.

"I just watched God raise my baby from the dead," Kellie explained. "What could I possibly fear? God will protect him from pneumonia. He will not leave him brain damaged."

Doctors could find no evidence of pneumonia or brain damage.

Back home, Brad and Kellie stood in the nursery watching their sleeping baby. "I learned something through this experience that you probably already knew from your years in the military," Kellie said.

"What's that?" Brad asked.

"Courage isn't the absence of fear. It's trusting God and standing in faith through it."

"That's true," Brad agreed. "What most people don't understand is that we're all in a war. There is a terrorist on the loose whose goal is to kill our children, and that terrorist is the devil. As Christians, we war with our words and we war with our faith. We have to get as radical as Moses and demand, 'Let my children go!'"

Today David Domby is a bright and joyful child. Blonde hair glistening in the sun and eyes sparkling with laughter, he is full of energy and good health. He is, in fact, just the way Kellie imagined him only moments before God raised him from death to life.

It is a fairy tale ending after all.

Which is only right if you're a child of the King.

The Seed of the Righteous

A frigid wind rattled the windows late that night in January 1970 as Henrietta Clementson gave up on sleep and crawled out of bed, careful not to wake her husband. Wrapping herself in an old quilt, its soft folds bringing her little comfort, she settled into a chair, her mood as dark as the night. In all her forty-eight years, Henrietta had never felt so...empty.

Why should she feel empty when her life was full and brimming over? She'd enjoyed a happy marriage for twenty-eight years, a union that had produced four wonderful children. Both her parents, who adored her, lived nearby. She and her family were members of an Anglican church where she'd been christened at six weeks old, and where she'd been confirmed at the age of twelve. Yet Henrietta felt as though she'd crawled into a deep and dark abyss from which she could never escape.

One of her sons had dated a wonderful girl for the past couple of years. Alive and vibrant one minute, she'd been killed in a car wreck the next. Tears streaming down her face, Henrietta pictured the young woman's familiar smile and sparkling eyes, hidden now behind the cold veil of death. Henrietta had expected to see those eyes in years to come looking back at her from the faces of her grandchildren. Knowing now she never would, she felt a loss so deep it threatened to sweep her into an abyss of grief she could never escape. It was as though she'd lost one of her own children... or even something more.

What's happening to me? Henrietta wondered, suddenly awakening to a void in her life she'd never known was there. It seemed this terrible event had opened a kind of sinkhole in her own soul through which she'd fallen. *Where did it come from? Perhaps more important, what would fill it?*

During the dark hours of the night, Henrietta dosed off to sleep. As the sun crept over the horizon, she awoke to the sound of her own weeping.

A few days later, the weather warmed and Henrietta carried a basket of laundry to the backyard. Sheets snapped in the wind as she hung them on the clothesline in the warm sun. Thinking of nothing more than the scent of fresh laundry in the breeze, unbidden words floated through her mind.

If you had one wish for your life above anything else, what would it be?

"To know God," Henrietta answered aloud.

The moment those words escaped her lips, Henrietta admitted the truth of them. Although she'd been in church her whole life, she didn't know God. She knew *about* God. She knew the liturgy. She knew the hymns. She revered God. But there was a chasm as deep between her and God as there was now between her and her son's girlfriend who'd crossed the barrier of death.

Lifting the empty laundry basket, Henrietta turned to go back inside the house. Before she reached the door, she stopped at the sound of a voice, although there was no one around.

"Go, look for your Bible," the voice instructed. *"Find your Bible. Read your Bible. Spend time in unhurried prayer."*

That afternoon, she found her Bible.

The following morning, she opened it to the book of John and began reading. She spent time in unhurried prayer. As days passed, Henrietta became sure of one thing: If she wanted to know God, she had to surrender to Him.

Surrender. The word carried a sense of finality. She'd been in church her whole life, and no one had ever talked about surrendering to God. *What if I surrender and lose all my friends?* she thought. *I have a husband and four children. What if I surrender and God sends me to China?*

She didn't know the answers to those questions, but as days passed, she realized that the emptiness in her life was a God-sized hole. Only God could change the dark abyss into a place of light and love. And without surrendering, what hope did she have for eternity?

One morning during her prayer time, Henrietta had a vision. She saw herself standing on the side of a boat, looking down into deep, black water. Without warning, she jumped.

That's what God wants me to do! she realized. *He wants me to jump into the deep waters with Him! He wants my total surrender, nothing less.*

She didn't contemplate the decision any longer. She'd already waited forty-eight years, so…she jumped.

"Jesus," she said out loud, "as of this minute, I give my life to You!"

That instant, Henrietta Clementson changed. Not only did she change into a new creature in Christ, but the very atmosphere of the room seemed charged with power. Goose bumps raised the hair on her body as she sensed a Presence in the room.

For the first time in her life, Henrietta experienced the presence of Jesus in every area of her being—spirit, soul, and body. That holy presence was so divine that she knew that this was what every human since the beginning of time searched for and ached for. This was what people used drugs and alcohol to try and mimic.

There was nothing like it on earth.

Living in the Light

Henrietta's experience with God was so life-changing that she crawled from bed at night, not to weep, but to ponder it. As months passed, the change in her was evident. She found a Bible study that she attended on Wednesday mornings. She hungered for the Word of God. Each time the woman leading the Bible study mentioned the name of Jesus, tears streamed down Henrietta's face.

Her family wanted to know what had happened, and she tried to wrap words around her experience. "You don't need to be fanatical," her parents urged with concern.

For Henrietta, the only downside to her new birth experience was that there was a chasm between her and her husband that she didn't know how to bridge. She was now in one kingdom, and he was in another. One night when she left her bed to be with the Lord, her husband, Jerry, followed her.

"I don't understand what's happened," he said.

Henrietta tried to explain it.

"Honey, I've known this stuff all my life," he said. Crawling onto the sofa, he put his head in her lap. "Where *are you?*" he asked.

What Jerry had known all his life mentally, his wife had now experienced spiritually. Like Henrietta only months before, he didn't understand that you cannot access God through knowledge. You cannot know God mentally, because God is a Spirit.

Henrietta read in the Bible where Jesus said, *"Most assuredly, I say to you, unless one is born again, he cannot see the kingdom of God"* (John 3:3). She understood that being born again meant diving into the deep waters of God and surrendering your life to Him.

She tried talking about it to her pastor, but he didn't understand. During services she listened to the boys' choir, all starched and lovely. They sang about God, but their eyes were dead. They didn't know Him!

Worse—far worse—her children didn't know Him.

She'd raised them in church. Like her, they knew *about* God. But they weren't toddlers any longer; they were grown. As a parent she'd failed to give them the most important thing in life—Jesus.

Although she'd prayed with passion for their salvation, three years after her own new birth experience, none of Henrietta's family was born again. She read in the Bible about what Jesus said about fasting. He didn't say, *"If you fast,"* she realized. He said, *"When you fast...."*

Determined for a breakthrough, Henrietta fasted for twenty-four days while praying for her family. Within nine months, her mother, father, husband, and all four children were radically saved, having surrendered their lives to Jesus.

A transformed Jerry and Henrietta ministered in Faith Alive Weekends while their children shared the gospel with others. For eight years, Henrietta and two of her sons fasted every Sunday evening through Tuesday morning.

A Heritage of Faith

As years passed, Henrietta followed the instructions the Holy Spirit gave her while hanging out the laundry in January of 1970. Every morning, rain or shine, she crawled out of bed, grabbed a mug of coffee and her Bible, and wrapped up in a blanket where she spent two hours in unhurried prayer.

As she grew in the Lord, Henrietta learned two things that put a question mark in her mind. First, she learned that the seed— or offspring—of the righteous are blessed. That meant that her children and grandchildren were blessed by the Lord because of her faith and prayers. She also learned that God does nothing on earth apart from the prayers of the saints.

She'd prayed her family into the kingdom. But the real question was: Who'd prayed *her* into the kingdom?

Henrietta was in her seventies before she learned the answer. She discovered that her ancestors on both sides were French Huguenots. On her father's side, one of her ancestors was John Lewis, who fled from Protestant persecution in Ireland. Traveling to America, he settled in the Shenandoah Valley and started the first church in his home. He was such a powerful Christian influence on the settlers that for fifteen years there had been no need for a prison.

On her mother's side, Henrietta was descended from Daniel Guerrant, whose father was martyred for his faith in France. Refusing to recant his faith in Christ, he was tortured to death. His children, one of whom was Daniel, were smuggled out of the country in potato sacks onto a ship on which they escaped to the New World.

Another of her ancestors, Thomas Christian, lived up to his name.

Her full name was Henrietta Christian Clementson. *I was named after this man!* Henrietta thought as she read through her genealogy. She was a descendant of a long line of born-again believers who'd long since gone home to heaven. Deuteronomy 7:9 came alive to her. "*Therefore know that the* LORD *your God, He is God, the faithful God who keeps covenant and mercy for a thousand generations with those who love Him and keep His commandments.*" God had honored their prayers and revealed Himself to her.

She was the seed—the descendent and recipient—of their righteous prayers!

On her eightieth birthday, Henrietta's family asked what they could do for her.

"I'd like all of you to come here and gather around me," she said. "I want to tell you what God has done in my life and what He will do in yours."

All thirty of Henrietta's immediate family members gathered around as she told them the story of her life and the lives of their ancestors. Then she explained all the blessings that are in store for the seed of the righteous.

Today, Henrietta Clementson is eighty-five years old and going strong. She mentors the young women in her church and is a righteous matriarch of her family. More important, she wakes every morning and sings praises to Jesus.

Jesus is the Living Savior.

He is the Seed of Righteousness.

Through Him, all the generations of the righteous are blessed.

Setting the Captives Free

Dark clouds shrouded the sun in southern California as John Ginty walked through Los Angeles toward Hollywood. Without warning, the heavens ripped apart and loosed drenching rain. Sprinting the last few blocks to his apartment, John changed into dry clothes as a radio weatherman blamed the uncharacteristic rain on El Niño. So what if the sun doesn't always shine in southern California? Back home in Syracuse, New York, his family still mucked their way through several feet of snow.

John stood in the center of his apartment and surveyed his empire. He had a suitcase, a pillow, an alarm clock, a clock radio, and three comic books. He didn't have a bed, a chair, or a dish. But John Ginty felt rich. At nineteen, he was living his dream. He'd purchased an airline ticket to Los Angeles, pocketed his life savings of $1,100, and left home. He had an apartment, a job at Office Max that would start in a couple of weeks, an agent, and a small part in his first movie. Shooting wouldn't start for several weeks, but he had enough money to survive until then.

It had all been so incredibly easy. Standing at the window, John watched the rain pound Hollywood like machine-gun fire. Somewhere on the streets outside, tires screeched and clawed at the waterlogged pavement as a frantic driver leaned on the horn. The sounds ricocheted off buildings and plate glass windows, sending a dark chill up John's spine. For a moment, he was back in Syracuse, hearing the same sickening screech, feeling the explosion of metal against metal and the sting of shattered glass.

The car wreck had happened months ago, but John slipped into the memory like it had happened yesterday. Another driver had run a stop sign and broadsided his car, melding it like hot plastic around him. As he'd crawled out the passenger side, John felt his whole world imploding. No bones were broken, no arteries slashed. "I'm okay...I'm okay..." he assured the bystanders who rushed to his aid.

In truth, however, John Ginty was far from okay. He was wounded in a way no X-ray could reveal and no doctor would notice. The already frayed filament of his faith had been severed. John Ginty no longer fully believed in God.

In the months leading up to the accident, a question about God's existence had buzzed in his mind like a gnat. He refused to vocalize it, but even so, it wouldn't go away. Raised in a Christian family and the eldest of four children, John had always assumed God was real because his parents believed it. He'd spent almost every Sunday of his childhood sitting in church, fidgeting alongside his brothers and sister, hearing about what God could do. But lately, he'd begun to wonder if what he'd heard was true. Maybe there was a more logical explanation for the world around him.

The drumming of the drops on his apartment window drew John back from the memory of those bleak months. Propping his pillow against the bare wall, he stretched out on the floor and opened a comic book. Better stick to the present. Syracuse, the car wreck, and the God who hadn't been there to stop it faded from his mind. He turned a brightly colored page and reminded himself it was time to start living his dream.

Finding the Answer

The next day the sun was back, smiling with approval as John walked the streets of Tinseltown embracing his new life. Ahead, he spotted a bevy of Scientologists eager to evangelize and sell their propaganda. Avoiding eye contact, he skirted the group and picked up his pace. Before he could fully congratulate himself on his escape, however, a young Japanese man carrying a clipboard apprehended him.

"Could I get you to take a few minutes and fill out a survey?" he asked

John sighed and envied his beloved comic book characters. *A cloak of invisibility would be handy right now. Oh well....*

The survey consisted of ten questions. Nine of them concerned family, family values, and community service. Question number ten asked, "If you had one question that you would like to have answered, what would it be?"

John answered that he would like to know if God existed.

"What if I told you that we could prove scientifically that there is a God?" the man asked. "Come with me, it will be real quick."

"No, thanks," John answered.

As John strode away, smiling once again at his newfound California freedom, the Japanese survey-taker stood watching until the crowds on the sidewalk swallowed him up and he disappeared from sight. John assumed the interaction was over, but the surveyor knew better. Whether John liked it or not, their relationship had just begun.

The next day John made a point of walking on the opposite side of the street. Even so, when he rounded the corner, he came face-to-face once again with his clipboard-carrying acquaintance from the day before. "Come with me, and I will prove the meaning of life!" he said, beaming a broad, pacific smile.

"No, thanks," John countered as the man trailed behind him, double-stepping to keep up with John's long-legged pace.

"It will be real quick...Just come with me...The meaning of life...Proof that God exists...." The words tugged at John with the innocence and persistence of a child determined to have his way. Clearly, this man would not give up until John listened to his spiel—whatever it was.

John surrendered to what seemed to be inevitable and followed him to a nearby home nestled between two fraternity houses. There a group of young people of various nationalities greeted him. Another Asian gentleman appeared and guided John through a maze of flow charts marked with peculiar mathematical equations. He finished his presentation with the confidence of a teacher who had proven his point.

"So you see," he said as he revealed the final equation, "that life equals love!"

"Wow!" John murmured, letting out a long breath. "That's incredible!"

It was more than incredible. It seemed to be the very answer he'd been searching for when he left home. The whole thing was pure logic.

"We're about to make dinner," the teacher said. "Stay and eat with us and we can visit."

After a pleasant meal, the group urged John to go with them to Chino Hills and spend the weekend. He frowned as he considered the idea. Somehow the few minutes he had intended to donate to the man with the clipboard had already turned into hours. Now they were about to turn into days.

Initially, John resisted. Something about it didn't seem quite right. But his new acquaintances gathered around him, their multi-hued faces benign yet determined, insisting he join them for their weekend retreat; John acquiesced. For better or worse, it seemed like the easiest thing to do.

No Way Out

Back home, his mother, Toni, woke from a disturbing dream and awakened her husband, Sean. "Something's wrong with John," she said. "We need to pray."

Toni had devoted her life to raising and protecting children—her own as well as the foster kids who, over the years, had filled the Ginty house until they spilled from every room. She and Sean had loved them all, sacrificing their time, their savings, and even their physical strength to make sure each child grew up in the nurture and admonition of the Lord.

Toni had always been fiercely protective of each one of them. Her beloved John was no exception. She knew how to pray, and she knew how to fight. Those who knew her best would be tempted to pity any poor devil that dared lay a finger on her kids.

She may have felt better about John after she and Sean prayed for him that night, but she wasn't foolish enough to think the danger had passed. She continued to wrestle the powers of darkness in her private times of prayer. Toni had no intention of letting the devil snatch John away and use him for his own dark purposes. John was destined to serve Jesus, and death itself couldn't stop her from seeing to it that destiny was fulfilled.

It didn't occur to John that once he reached the retreat site, he might never return to the Hollywood life he'd once anticipated. *I'll be away a couple of days, at most,* he figured, *then I'll go back.* But as Saturday melted into Sunday...and then into Monday...a subtle, constant pressure to stay longer weakened John's resolve. *What's the hurry?* he found himself wondering. After all, his questions about God were finally being answered, and the world was making sense again. He agreed to stay a week.

That week turned into two and the second week turned into three. Before he knew it, John had lost his job, his apartment, his agent, and his role in a movie. Somehow, the soft-spoken, smiling group that had taken him in had also ended up with all of John's money.

He had no way out.

One morning he woke very early and tiptoed into a meeting room uninvited to see what was happening. The entire group was bowing in worship to photographs of Sun Myung Moon and his wife.

Life on the Run

John phoned home and described what he'd seen to his parents. "Do you know who he is?" Sean asked. "Sun Myung Moon is a Korean man who believes he's the second coming of Christ incarnate. He's head of the Unification church—the largest cult in the world. Dear heavens, John, you've gotten tangled up with the *Moonies!*"

John hoped his dad had overreacted but soon realized he hadn't. Sure enough, he found out that the nice people around him did, indeed, believe that Sun Myung Moon was a second Messiah. He was sent by God, they explained to John, for the purpose of completing the mission the first Messiah, Jesus Christ, had failed to accomplish—the creation of a perfect family on earth.

John wasn't sure he bought the doctrine, but he was enjoying the company of his new friends. So what if he had a few theological differences with them? Tucking a box of key chains, wind chimes, and other cheap trinkets under his arm, John ducked into a van filled with his fellow Moonies and headed for the streets of L.A. to spend the day fund-raising for the cause.

John spent the next few months crisscrossing the southwest in a surreal fund-raising trek that took him through California to the Grand Canyon, through Idaho and Yellowstone Park to Boulder, Colorado, and ended in Denver. With every day that passed, John felt a growing sense of uneasiness.

When he asked what would happen next, he was told that from Denver the group would return to California. From California they would go to Japan and Russia before reaching Korea. What was supposed to happen in Korea bristled the hair on the back of his neck. There, each group member would be paired with a mate, usually from another country, and in a group ceremony consisting of five hundred to one thousand couples, they would be married.

"An arranged marriage?" John asked, his voice ascending an octave.

"We must create the perfect family," the leader explained.

How am I ever going to get out of this? John wondered.

Back in Syracuse, John's family and church prayed for him regularly. Sean and Toni had learned there were cult experts who could be hired to help John escape, but they cost thousands of dollars—money the Gintys didn't have. They determined to trust God and believe that somehow He would personally show John the way out.

Breaking the Death Grip

The night before John's group planned to leave Denver, they walked out of a restaurant to find their van vandalized. Someone had smashed the windows. Oddly enough, however, nothing in the van had been stolen. Even the bank bag with all their money remained safely in plain sight. *How strange!* John thought.

Getting the windows repaired meant staying in Denver one extra day. The next morning, John walked through downtown selling trinkets when he noticed a newspaper. The front page featured a picture of a man with a gruff expression. The caption read: *Cult Cop.*

Glancing behind him to make sure no one was watching, John slipped two quarters into the slot, pulled out a paper, and scanned the article. The man's name was Mark Roggeman. He was internationally renowned for getting people out of cults. He was most experienced with the Unification Church, also known as the Moonies. Mr. Roggeman lived in Denver. His contact information was included. "If you need help, or know someone who does, call now," the article urged.

John folded the paper and hid it in his backpack. That afternoon, he took a deep breath and dialed the number. Mark Roggeman answered the phone and directed John to a nearby Christian bookstore. After spending the afternoon talking to the store owner, John knew what he had to do. He went back to the group to gather his meager belongings and leave.

If John thought that would be easy, he was wrong. When he got back to the van, the group leader confronted him and informed him he couldn't go.

"Look, you said I could leave anytime," John answered. "So I'm leaving now."

"Get in the van; we'll talk about it when we reach Los Angeles."

John shook his head, grabbed his bag and pillow, and turned to walk away. Before he could take the first step, a force from behind sent him stumbling. "What are you doing? Get off me!" he demanded. The once-smiling leader had abandoned his pleasant demeanor and now clung to John's back with a death grip. "You're coming back with us," he growled.

John threw his full weight backward and slammed his would-be captor full force against the van. "I'm leaving!" he shouted.

Bleeding but determined to do whatever was necessary to return John to the flock, the leader tightened his grip. "No!" he said, "you'll come back with us!"

In desperation, John bolted across the parking lot, trying—and failing—to shake himself free. He could only think of one other thing to do. He fell over backwards onto the pavement, pinning the relentless leader beneath him. Still, he wouldn't let go. At six feet two inches tall and weighing 200 pounds, John could hold his own in most situations. How was it he couldn't escape the fanatical man on his back?

A couple walking by paused to gape at the sight. "Is everything all right?" they asked.

"No, it isn't," John called, still trying to get free. "Could you call the police?"

"Yes!"

"No! No! We're family!" the cult leader shouted.

"No, we're not!" John assured them.

When the police car squealed to a stop, the officer watched, perplexed, as the diminutive leader—somewhat the worse for wear—loosened his grip and slid from John's back like a child scrambling down from a tree.

"I need to leave this group," John explained to the mystified policeman.

"If he goes, he'll be homeless!" the leader argued, knowing there was a law against homelessness in Denver.

"Well…." the officer pondered the situation. "Where will you go?"

As if on cue, a van pulled up. John could hardly believe his eyes. It was the bookstore owner! "I'm his uncle, officer," he said, "and he's coming with me."

John picked up his bag and pillow and hurried to the van. Midstride, the Japanese leader jumped him from behind again. But when the officer pulled his baton, the leader had a change of heart and decided to let John go free.

Free at Last

John spent the next month in Mark Roggeman's home looking for a job in Denver and finding a roommate. During that time, he pondered the events that surrounded his escape from the Moonies, and he realized that there were too many coincidences to ignore. The smashed van windows that had led to the extra day in Denver…a day when a newspaper—one that only existed for three months—ran a front page story with the headline *Cult Cop!*

What were the odds of Mark Roggeman just happening to be home to answer his call? And what about the couple who happened by and called the police? And the bookstore owner arriving at exactly the right moment?

John stood one morning in Mark Roggeman's kitchen and marveled at the chain of events that had brought him there. Gaining the help of a cult expert could cost thousands of dollars; John got help from one of the nation's leading cult experts for free. Who else could have arranged that but God?

There was no doubt in John Ginty's mind anymore that God existed. Nor was there any doubt that Jesus was the Son of God or that the Bible was true.

It took a few more years—six, to be exact—for the rest of John's life to line up with that revelation. During those years, while his parents continued praying, John lived the party life. But the day his dad called and told him his mother had been diagnosed with terminal cancer and wasn't expected to live, he realized not only how much he loved her but how much he owed her.

A few months later, John called his father to tell him he'd had a change of plans. "I'm coming home to take care of my mother," he said.

For the next seven months, John Ginty laid down his life, caring and praying for the woman who'd laid down her life praying for him. The days, weeks, and months he spent with her, though full of pain and difficulty for them both, were tender and precious to him; their reunion a celebration of life instead of death.

When John said his final good-byes to his mother, she knew beyond a doubt that God had answered her prayers. John had become the man she'd seen by faith when circumstances screamed a different message. They parted with the assurance that one day they would be united with Jesus.

Although John's mother is home with the Lord now, her prayers are alive and powerful in the lives of her children...and her children's children. They are still releasing the power that sets the captives free.

Worth the Wait

Giggling first-graders romped through the fresh spring grass like puppies released from a cage under Missy Matthys' watchful gaze. Some scattered to the swings, others to the teeter-totters. A few girls with bouncing ponytails played jump rope; nearby boys kicked a soccer ball. Even after seven years of teaching first grade, Missy never tired of the moving maze of color and laughter called recess...and she never stopped dreaming of the day she'd see her own child skipping out to join the fun.

After school, Missy drove home and started dinner as usual. Slicing fresh tomatoes, she heard the garage door open as her husband, Russ, arrived home. No need to hurry getting the food on the table. It would still be a while before Russ's lanky frame appeared in the doorway. The flocks of neighborhood children who always greeted him would ambush him as soon as he stepped out of the car.

Sticking her head outside, Missy saw the driveway littered with bicycles. Clearly, her husband was a kid magnet.

"Hi, Mr. Russ!" one of the kids said, offering Russ a high five.

"Hey," Russ answered, "what's happening in school?"

Missy shook her head with a smile and went back to the kitchen. The aroma of warm bread filled the air when Russ darted inside, water dripping from his face. "Hey, where's my squirt gun?" he asked.

"Why?" Missy quizzed with a grin.

"We're having a squirt gun fight and I can't find mine."

Setting the timer for the rolls, Missy traipsed outside in search of the elusive gun. Meanwhile a drenched Russ grabbed the water hose. Her heart lurched as she watched Russ play with the kids. "Don't you have a birthday coming up?" he asked one of the boys.

"It's today!" the child cried, happy that Russ remembered.

Blinking back tears, Missy went inside. She and Russ had yearned to have children for years. They'd even picked out names for their first son and daughter before they were married. *Isaac Allen* and *Rebecca Rose*.... The very thought of those names pricked Missy's heart like two tiny thorns on a perfect flower, and she felt again the familiar pain of her childlessness.

She and Russ had spent almost five years now hoping and praying that they would conceive. During those years, they'd gone through a battery of infertility tests, even gathering paperwork about adoption and investigating infertility drugs. But through it all, they had sensed the Lord telling them to do the one thing they didn't want to do anymore.

Wait.

If it hadn't been for their pastors and good friends, they might not have obeyed that command. Even if they had, they wouldn't have known what to do while they were waiting. Their pastors and church members helped them learn to pray and speak God's Word over their situation in faith.

Missy looked up to see Russ coming through the door, brown hair soaked and blue eyes sparkling. Apparently the water fight was over. "What happened?" she quipped. "Did the other kids have to go home?"

As Russ ambled away hunting for a towel, Missy set two plates on the table. *Someday, I'll be setting places for four,* she thought. *Soon, Lord…please, let it be soon.*

Rebecca Rose

Sure enough, a few months later, Russ and Missy got the news they'd been waiting five years to hear. Missy was pregnant. Thrilled beyond belief, they busied themselves picking colors and preparing the nursery for the baby's arrival. Outside the nursery window, the autumn leaves joined their celebration, dancing and sparkling in reds and yellows. Even when the leaves grew weary and fell to the ground to nap under the late November snow, the sparkle of lights strung early for Christmas kept the mood outside as festive as it was inside. Nothing, it seemed—not even a Minnesota winter—could chill Russ and Missy's enthusiasm.

On December 2, Missy was scheduled to get her first ultrasound. The day before, Missy noticed a little spotting, reminiscent of her monthly cycle. That evening, friends from church, Keith and Kristen, dropped off a CD of praise music and a note while Russ and Missy were out. Home later that evening, they spent two hours praising God before going to bed. Drifting off to sleep, Missy's heart skipped with joy at the thought of seeing her baby for the first time.

Hours later, she awoke in agony. Something was clearly wrong. "Russ!" she said, shaking her groggy husband in alarm. "Wake up. We need to pray!"

The next morning, Missy looked pale and exhausted when they arrived at the doctor's office. "How are you doing?" the doctor asked.

Neither Russ nor Missy could find words to answer the question. With trembling, tender hands, Russ lifted the tiny form of their daughter, Rebecca Rose, from the dark coffin of his pocket.

The dream that had taken five years to conceive was dead.

At home, Russ and Missy collapsed in each other's arms as the phone jangled with calls from jubilant family and friends wanting to know the result of Missy's ultrasound. Again and again, Russ retold—and relived—the tragedy of the previous hours. When Kristen called and asked how he was doing, he unleashed his anger.

"How do you think I'm doing?" he said, his voice ragged with tears and rage. "I'm dealing with two huge losses. I'm dealing with the loss of our child, and I'm furious at being betrayed by God."

"Russ," she gasped, "God didn't do this!"

"What do you mean?"

"The Bible says in John 10:10 that the thief is the one who comes to steal, to kill, and to destroy. Jesus came that we might have abundant life. The thief is the devil, Russ. He's the one to blame."

The words slammed against Russ's heart with a shock of spiritual power and brought the faith that had died with his daughter gasping back to life. "You're right," he said, still sobbing, "God didn't do this!"

The Good Fight of Faith

Over the next few months, Keith and Kristen helped Russ and Missy regather their spiritual weapons and strike back at the thief who had laid them low. The first thing they did was search the Bible to find out what God says about the children of His people. Next, based on those Scriptures, they wrote a prayer of petition and agreement. They began confessing the Scriptures daily.

> *So you shall serve the LORD your God, and He will bless your bread and your water. And I will take sickness away from the midst of you. No one shall suffer miscarriage or be barren in your land; I will fulfill the number of your days.*
>   (Exodus 23:25–26)

> *You shall be blessed above all peoples; there shall not be a male or female barren among you or among your livestock.*
>   (Deuteronomy 7:14)

> *He grants the barren woman a home, like a joyful mother of children. Praise the LORD!*   (Psalm 113:9)

When the doctor explained that they'd lost Rebecca because of a problem with Missy's placenta, Missy wrote her confession of faith and spoke it daily. "A godly seed has been planted firmly in my womb," she said. "I'm well able to carry children. I've been designed by God to do it. I have a protected womb and a perfect placenta."

As Russ and Missy learned the concept of sowing and reaping, they began sowing into the lives of children. They gave gifts to children, hosted baby showers, and babysat for friends.

Even so, the months turned into years with no apparent answer to Russ and Missy's prayers. Their dreams of hearing the gleeful shrieks of toddlers and the clomp of clumsy, little feet went unfulfilled and their home remained silent. Their hopes of pulling a high chair to the kitchen table and setting extra plates were disappointed. Night after night, Russ and Missy ate dinner alone.

As if that wasn't enough, when Missy approached 40, a relative suggested she had already passed her childbearing prime. "Honey," she said, "your eggs are *old!*"

Missy knew she couldn't let her concern go unanswered, so she took the matter to the Lord in prayer. He reminded her of Psalm 92:14, "*They shall still bring forth fruit in old age*" (KJV).

As Russ and Missy dug through the Bible seeking more ammunition for their fight, they learned that faith without works is dead. "We need to be careful to act on our faith and obey the Lord in whatever He tells us to do," Russ said.

"Okay," Missy agreed. "Let's start *expecting* to be expecting. We left the nursery in a shambles after losing Rebecca. I'm going to act on my faith by finishing the nursery."

As Russ and Missy sought the Lord about changes they should make, one of the first things He addressed was their attitude. They made a decision to be joyful. No longer would they allow Missy's monthly cycle to send them spiraling into depression. They chose, instead, to rejoice and believe that—no matter what—they were closer to having their baby.

"We also have to forgive everyone who has said thoughtless or unkind things," Russ told Missy. "Faith works by love and unforgiveness will hinder our faith."

Confident the Lord was leading them to victory, they acted on every prompting of the Spirit they sensed in their heart. When Missy felt led to change her diet to include more foods like broccoli and yams, she did it. Their meals soon became an array of vibrant colors and healthy food. When the Lord told Missy that they should buy a minivan for their growing family, Russ immediately took her shopping and bought one.

Every step along the way, they were in agreement. But when Missy told Russ the Lord had instructed her to buy a stroller and walk around the neighborhood, Russ balked. Acting on faith was fine; pushing an empty stroller around in public was not okay. Russ didn't even want to buy a stroller.

Missy knew better than to get cranky about the situation. She had enough experience with both God and Russ to trust the conflict would soon be resolved.

The Next Step

Weeks later, Russ arrived home from work and announced, "We need to buy a stroller!" When they went shopping, they found dozens to choose from, yet they were both drawn to the same one—a double stroller!

Not only was it perfect for a growing family, it was a perfect expression of their faith. After all, they were praying for more than one child. Why not go ahead and prepare for two?

One afternoon not long after that, Missy sensed the Lord urging her to take the next step of faith. In one seat of the double stroller she set a Bible; her purse rested in the other. Pushing the stroller down the street, joy washed over Missy in waves so great that she laughed, sang, and praised the Lord.

Dialing her cell phone, she called Russ. "Pushing this stroller has brought joy that I'd never imagined," she said. "This one act of obedience has boosted my faith!"

Oddly enough, however, Russ and Missy still saw no answer to their prayers.

Searching the Bible for answers, they realized that the devil had always warred against the children of the righteous. The first patriarch, Abraham, was one hundred years old when he received his son of promise. He stood in faith for a son for twenty-five years before the enemy of barrenness fled from his life. If necessary, Russ and Missy were prepared to do the same. They would fight—and win the war for their children—to the very end.

Three years after losing Rebecca, Russ and Missy took a tour to Israel. For them, the highlight of the trip was not Jerusalem. It was not the temple wall. Their own personal journey took them to Shiloh. It was there that the Bible describes a barren woman, Hannah, praying for a child. Because of her prayers, her first son—the prophet Samuel—was born.

Walking through the rocky ruins, Russ and Missy found the site of the former Holy of Holies. There, where Hannah received an answer to her prayers, they too cried out to God for their children.

Back home in the United States, Russ and Missy attended a service where the speaker called everyone who wanted to conceive to come forward for prayer. Unwilling to leave any stone unturned, they went forward and received prayer.

Still there was no evidence of change.

In January of the following year, Russ and Missy went cross-country skiing. The sun was warm on Missy's face as she glided past trees laden with fresh snow. Inhaling the crisp, cold air, she could almost hear her children's voices as they poled their way across the soft snow to their dad. She doubled over from the pain of wanting them.

Up ahead, Russ heard the air split with the sound of his wife's scream.

"Devil, get your hands off of me!"

Russ slid to a stop at the fury of her words. *Oh boy*, he thought, looking around to see how many people were listening.

Missy spiked her ski poles in the ground and continued to shout. "We *have* our children by faith! Devil, get your hands *off!* They *belong to us!*"

Missy finished screaming and skied away.

Three weeks later, she was pregnant.

"We can't let up on our warfare now," Russ told Missy. "We'll continue with our Scripture confessions, and I'll lay hands on you and pray over you and the baby every night. We're not going to lose this child."

True to his word, Russ prayed over Missy and the baby every night. The night before her first ultrasound, the same symptoms that Missy experienced when she miscarried returned. Pain gripped her, and then she began to bleed.

"We will not give in to fear," Russ said. "We're going to fight the good fight of faith."

The next morning, the ultrasound revealed a live baby girl in Missy's womb.

On November 11, 2004, Lissa Faith Matthys filled the emptiness in Russ and Missy's home and the ache in their arms. Two years later, on November 1, 2006, Isaac Allen Matthys was born.

Recently, Russ pulled into the garage after work as neighborhood kids followed him on their bicycles. After visiting with the children, Russ and Missy loaded Lissa and Isaac into the double stroller. Bright green sprigs of grass waved in the gentle breeze at the nearby park. Giggling children ran from swings to the jungle gym to play and, once again, became the moving maze of color and sound Missy marveled over every year. But this year, she and Russ no longer stood watching on the sidelines. This year, sailing skyward in the swings were their very own children, the ones they had fought for ten long years. As the swings swished back and forth, higher and higher, Lissa and Isaac laughed so hard they gasped for air.

It had been a long battle for Russ and Missy Matthys, but one thing was clear: The children they won were worth every moment of the war; every second of the wait.

The Most Powerful Force on Earth

The moon was cloaked behind dark clouds, the midnight sky as black as a sin-stained conscience by the time thirteen-year-old Nathanael Wolf crept into the house. Careful to avoid creaking floorboards, he tiptoed past his mother's bedroom. For a moment all was silent and his shoulders sagged with relief. *Home free!* he thought.

Not quite. He lifted his foot to take one more soundless step and froze as soft sobs broken by gentle murmurs floated into the hallway. His mother was praying again. Nate stopped cold and the hair on the back of his neck stood on end at the sound.

He knew what he'd see when he looked into her room. He'd witnessed the scene countless times before. His mother would be kneeling on the floor, crying out to God, pleading for Him to intervene in her son's life. It didn't matter what time he snuck home, that's what Nate usually found her doing. Sighing, he slunk to his bedroom. Before morning she would know everything he'd done—what he drank and the drugs he'd used.

Nate clenched his jaw in defiance. It didn't matter how many times God ratted on him, he wasn't going to serve Him. Yes, he'd given his life to Jesus when he was four years old. He still remembered the time a missionary offered an altar call for those who felt the Lord tugging them into ministry. Five-year-old Nate had been the only one who'd gone forward. The missionary had laid hands on him and prayed.

But a lot of things had changed since then. Nate was no longer a naive, obedient kindergartener. He was a hell-raising adolescent. God knew it, too. Nate was certain of that. The way he figured it, God had some kind of cosmic video camera that recorded everything you did wrong. When you died and showed up for judgment, God pressed the *Play* button.

Nate's videotape had already captured enough incriminating evidence to bust him for eternity. He didn't see any point even trying to be good anymore. Given all the bad things he'd done, His heavenly Father must be as furious with him as his earthly father was. Nate couldn't do anything to please him either. He could only hope God's wrath would be less painful than his dad's.

In his room, Nate tried to shake the haunting echo of his mother's voice. *Let her pray*, he thought as he crawled into bed and pulled the cover up over his head. *It won't do any good.*

A Prayer of Promise

Wednesday nights were church nights at the Wolf house. Always. Without fail. No matter how much Nate protested. So that week, he wanted to dance for joy when he got a reprieve. His uncle was in town for a visit, and for once they were going to skip the Wednesday night service.

As they drove to the impromptu family reunion, Nate's mother sat rigid in the front seat and fidgeted with the handle of her purse. "For some reason, I don't feel good about going," she said.

"I don't either," Nate's dad admitted. "But...family is family, so we'd better go."

At first, the concerns seemed unfounded. The visit started with the usual pleasantries; then, without warning, the atmosphere changed. Nate's uncle grew agitated, reeling from the effects of eight different drugs no one in the family realized he had taken. When his rage flared into threats of violence, a deadly drama unfolded.

"I'm going to get a gun and kill you all," he declared to the horrified family.

The events that followed tumbled together in a blur before Nate's terrified eyes—a frantic call to the sheriff...the sight of a holstered gun and an officer warning his wild-eyed uncle to settle down...the rush of relief when the sheriff's car rolled away, and it seemed for a moment that the crisis had passed...Nate's uncle erupting again, ranting about a murder he claimed he'd committed...Nate's mother asking him to calm down. Then the unthinkable happened.

In one fluid movement, the uncle grabbed a knife, pulled Nate's mother into a headlock and stabbed her in the throat. Blood pulsed twelve inches from her carotid artery with each beat of her heart as he stabbed her again and again. Her heart stopped as the blade pierced it.

Nate's dad fought to free her and became the next victim as his brother turned the knife on him, cutting his throat from ear to ear. Desperate to stop the slaughter, Nate grabbed a fireplace poker and swung it full force against his uncle's head. Nate's dad took the opportunity to scoop up his bleeding wife and escape. Nate scrambled out of the house behind them and called for help.

"Everything's going dark and I feel so cold," Nate's mother whispered as she hemorrhaged copious amounts of blood. "I'm dying. Nate, promise me you'll serve the Lord."

"Lord, I'll serve You if You'll spare my mom!" Nate prayed. "Now Mom, promise me that you'll live!"

By the time the ambulance reached the hospital, no more blood pulsated from her neck. Her carotid artery was whole. There was no wound in her heart. No fatal injuries.

Nate knew that God had answered his prayer. But, even so, he reneged on his rash promise. Jaw clenched and eyes hard as flint, he refused to serve the Lord.

A Death Wish

As days turned to months, and months to years, Nate became a prisoner behind the bars of his own hardened heart. There were only two ways of escape and he knew it. He could break free by choosing life in service to God; or he could end it all by choosing death. Still defiant, Nate chose death.

Three years after the ordeal with his uncle, Nate arrived home drunk one night and found his parents waiting for him.

"I don't want to have anything to do with either of you!" he shouted.

"What about the Lord?" his mother asked with a stricken look on her face.

Looking up to heaven, Nate made an obscene gesture. "God, I hate You. Jesus, stay out of my life. I *won't* do what You want me to do."

Not long afterwards, Nate's girlfriend broke up with him. Drunk and in despair, he drove through town at 120 miles per hour.

"You're going to hit someone and we'll die!" his friend shouted, gripping the dashboard with white knuckles.

"Yeah, we're going to die tonight!" Nate howled.

Somehow, they plowed through five stoplights without hitting anyone.

At home, Nate decided to finish the job. Sliding six bullets into a .357 Magnum, he pulled the hammer back and put the gun in his mouth.

Before he pulled the trigger, every sermon he'd ever heard about hell flooded his mind. He felt terrified...and trapped. Pulling the gun out of his mouth, he put it away.

Liquid Love

At the gym a few days later, Nate sat in the weight room. Around him, other men worked in teams, acting as spotters and barking words of encouragement to each other as they hefted weight-laden bars. Nate turned his back on them all and reached for a set of dumbbells. He preferred to work out alone.

"*Nathanael.*" Nobody ever called him Nathanael. Putting his weights down, he turned to look over his shoulder.

Strange. No one was there. He glanced around to see who might have spoken to him, but nobody was looking his way.

"*Nathanael, I love you.*"

This time the words washed over him in waves like liquid love. The presence of God fell over him with the heaviness of glory.

"*I want you to go to the Philippine Islands.*"

Me? Go to the Philippines? Nate shook his head at the thought. The youth group at his church was planning a summer mission trip there, but he had never entertained the idea of joining them.

"God, I don't want to go," he said. "First of all, You picked the wrong guy. I use drugs and alcohol. I'm not pure morally. Send Mike. Send Peggy. Send Annie."

"*I'm sending them, but I want you to go, too.*"

"I don't want to go. I don't want to serve You."

Nate already had his life mapped out. He planned on joining the Marines and then becoming a gunrunner in Africa. Going to the Philippines didn't fit his agenda.

"*No matter how far you run, no matter where you go—My love will be there waiting for you.*"

In that instant, Nate knew without a doubt that God wasn't mad at him. He knew that God didn't want to judge him. He knew that if he didn't serve God his life would be cut short.

God wasn't trying to control him; He was trying to save him.

As tears streamed down Nate's face, the guys in the weight room looked away, uncomfortable at the sight. But Nate didn't care. Driving home, he prayed and wept even more. "Lord, I ask that You forgive me of my sins."

Alone in his bedroom, Nate asked the Holy Spirit to help him pray. Then, kneeling on the floor the way he'd seen his mother do so many times, he poured out his grief to God. What seemed like moments later, he realized that he'd prayed for three hours.

As he stared at the clock in wonder and heard a gentle rap on his door. He looked up to see his mother set a Bible on his bedside table. "I want you to start reading this tomorrow," she said.

Transformation

Over the next three months, Nate read the New Testament twenty-seven times and prayed for three to five hours a day. Yet he still hungered for more of God.

"Mom, I want to learn about prayer," he said.

"You need to learn from Sister Stewart," she said, referring to an eighty-six-year-old widow in the church. "Sister Stewart is my prayer partner and has spent years praying for you."

Sister Stewart's eyes twinkled when she heard Nate's proposal. "I'll clean your house if you'll let me listen to you pray," he said.

Nate watched and listened as Sister Stewart settled into a chair with a world atlas beside her. Each prayer time, she prayed in the Spirit and then interpreted her prayers. Once, Nate heard her pray in deep intercession over an earthquake that would hit Mexico City. Months later when the earthquake hit, Nate wondered how many lives she'd saved. Another time, he listened in fascination as she prayed over a volcanic eruption on a remote island. When it hit the news, Nate thrilled to learn that everyone escaped to safety.

That summer, Nate traveled to the Philippine Islands with his youth group. Mustering up his courage, he preached for fifteen minutes on the streets.

Thirty-three people gave their hearts to Jesus.

When he returned home, Nate and some of the other youth in the church started holding all night prayer meetings. Nate's dad, touched by their sincerity, converted his garage into a prayer room.

After high school, Nate abandoned his plan to join the Marines and attended Bible College instead. Rather than running guns in Africa, he opted to smuggle Bibles, minister in Communist countries, and run from the secret police. He also became a husband, a father of four children, two girls and two boys, and pastor of Today's Church.

These days, whenever he can, Nate swings his leg over his Harley and hits the road to reach others whose hearts are as hardened as his once was. As Chapter President of the Seattle area Tribe of Judah Motorcycle Ministries, he roars across the countryside, bringing the gospel of God's love to 1 percent Motorcycle Clubs such as the Bandidos, Hell's Angels, and many other hardcore souls.

All in all, Nathanael's life in service to the Lord is a very good ride.

Left to himself, Nathanael would have missed that ride and chosen an early death. But the tenacious prayers of his mother and her friend, Sister Stewart, got in his way. Their prayers saved his life just as surely as his desperate cry to God once stopped a hemorrhage and healed his mother's carotid artery.

Prayer is the most powerful force on earth. That's one thing Nathanael Wolf will never doubt. He has seen it bring protection from a volcanic eruption. He has seen it provide safety in the midst of an earthquake. He has seen it heal his childhood wounds with liquid love and transform his life.

Every breath he takes is evidence that prayer changes everything.

Part Three

WINNING THE WAR FOR OUR CHILDREN

By Gina

Part Three

WINNING THE WAR FOR OUR CHILDREN

The evidence is clear: a spiritual war is raging over the children of believers. The stories in this book bear that out, and the Bible backs them up. It is a war that will continue until Jesus returns. And it is a war that we, as Christian parents, can win.

To do so, however, we must stop waiting for the devil to bring the battle to our doorstep. It's been said that the best defense is a good offense; and when it comes to raising and praying for our children, that more than anything else is what we need. We need to go on the offensive. Shaking off our peacetime mentality, we must cease being surprised at the devil's myriad assaults on our kids and develop a strategy that will put him on the defensive for a change.

How do we develop such a strategy?

We can start by changing the way we view our children, by seeing them as God sees them—not as victims of the moral and spiritual darkness of this age, but as up-and-coming victors called by God to put that darkness to flight. Fanning the flames of our faith with the pages of the Bible, we can dare to believe that we are raising up a generation of young saints like those the prophets foretold: young people who, because they *"know their God... shall be strong, and carry out great exploits"* (Daniel 11:32); kids like David and Daniel and Esther who are bold enough to slay the Goliaths the devil sends against them, strong enough to stand uncompromising and unharmed in the midst of the lion's den, and wise enough to beat wicked Haman at his own game.

That generation is coming. God has declared it, and the devil knows it's true. He has known it ever since the garden of Eden. It was there he first heard the chilling prophecy that has haunted him ever since he successfully tempted Adam and Eve. It was there he heard God say:

> *Because you have done this, you are cursed more than all cattle, and more than every beast of the field; on your belly you shall go, and you shall eat dust all the days of your life. And I will put enmity between you and the woman, and between your seed and her Seed; He shall bruise your head, and you shall bruise His heel.*   (Genesis 3:14–15)

Those words put in perspective the spiritual war that's being fought over our kids today. They reveal a truth too little understood by most Christian parents—that it is not the devil who has declared war on our children; it is God who has declared war on the devil. The Creator of the universe is the One who threw down the gauntlet by announcing in advance that the seed of the righteous would one day crush Satan under their feet.

Ever since that moment, the devil has been fighting to defend himself against the children of God's people. They are, in his eyes, the ultimate threat.

If you doubt it, read through the Bible and see how persistently and aggressively the devil has targeted them. Starting with Eve's first two sons, he wasted no time setting about to destroy Adam's offspring with moral corruption and physical danger. It was the devil himself who sent sin to crouch at the door of Cain's heart and incited him to murder his righteous brother. The plot was not hatched out of idle mischief, either. It was spawned by Satan's fear of what those two young men might one day do to him. It was a preemptive strike designed to keep their heels off his head.

And though it was the first such strike, it was not the last—nor was it the most vicious.

The Bible tells us about times when Satan so feared that a serpent-crushing deliverer was arising from among the children of God's people that he lashed out with the vengeance of a mass murderer to kill them all. Pharaoh and Herod might have been the puppet rulers who ordered all the Hebrew babies to be drowned in the river or slain by Roman swords, but the devil himself was pulling the strings.

The Generation the Devil Has Been Dreading

"But what does all that have to do with our children today?" you might ask. "Jesus was the *Seed* God was talking about in the Garden of Eden. He's the One with the power to defeat the devil, and through His death and resurrection, He's already done it."

That's true, but Jesus has given the church the responsibility of enforcing that defeat; and our children represent the church of the future. They loom on the devil's horizon as the next generation of overcomers,…and they may well be the ones Jesus has been waiting for—the generation of end-time believers who will finally make His enemies His footstool. (See Hebrews 1:13.) The devil knows it even if we don't: The little men and women of God who are now being tucked into beds and kissed good night by their Christian parents may turn out to be the ultimate fulfillment of New Testament declarations like these:

> *And it shall come to pass in the last days, says God, that I will pour out of My Spirit on all flesh; your sons and your daughters shall prophesy, your young men shall see visions, your old men shall dream dreams. And on My menservants and on My maidservants I will pour out My Spirit in those days; and they shall prophesy. I will show wonders in heaven above and signs in the earth beneath: blood and fire and vapor of smoke. The sun shall be turned into darkness, and the moon into blood, before the coming of the great and awesome day of the* LORD.   (Acts 2:17–21)

> *And the God of peace will crush Satan under your feet shortly.*   (Romans 16:20)

> *For whatever is born of God overcomes the world. And this is the victory that has overcome the world; our faith.*
> (1 John 5:4)

> *And they overcame him* [the devil] *by the blood of the Lamb and by the word of their testimony, and they did not love their lives to the death.*   (Revelation 12:11)

Granted, those verses can apply to every born-again believer. Everyone who makes Jesus their Lord has His overcoming power within them. But learning to use that power effectively takes time, training, and revelation.

That's why the children of believers—kids who've been raised up in the knowledge of God's Word and trained since they were toddlers in the truths of redemption—absolutely terrify the forces of darkness. Those children are beneficiaries of the spiritual knowledge their parents have passed along to them, and that knowledge boosts their capacity to exercise the spiritual authority God has given them. Those kids not only have the right to reign as kings on the earth because they are born-again believers themselves; they know how to exercise that right effectively because their parents taught them how.

Once we as Christian parents fully grasp that truth, we will devote ourselves more passionately to bringing up our children in the training and admonition of the Lord. We will be more serious about our responsibility to stand in faith on their behalf and wrestle against the principalities, powers, and rulers of the darkness of this age who strive to douse their spiritual light. We will fight for them with fresh fervor in prayer until they stand perfect and complete in all the will of God. (See Ephesians 6:4, 12; Colossians 4:12.)

Do you know what will happen when we Christian parents throughout the church begin to do that? The godly generation the devil has been dreading for six thousand years will emerge at last. He will finally be forced to face the massive army of believers he already knows is coming—the children of the righteous who are *ordained and trained to crush Satan under their feet.*

Stake Your Claim

Our kids *are* ordained to do that, you know. According to the Bible, they are predestined and set apart in advance to be disciples of the Lord Jesus Christ. That's why, when we pray for them, we can pray not only with great love and great hope, but with great faith as well. That's why, when our kids go astray, we don't have to be haunted by questions like…*What if my child chooses to reject Jesus? What if he refuses to answer God's call?*

The Bible assures us that because we are believers, God has already destined our children to be His. It promises us that if we will pray and believe, we can fully trust the Hound of Heaven to stay hot on their trail until they are caught, once and for all, in the tender net of God's love.

That doesn't mean, of course, that our children can be eternally saved by our faith alone. We cannot make them Christians by sprinkling water on their heads or dedicating them to God when they are babies. The New Testament plainly tells us that every individual must be born again by personal faith in the Lord Jesus Christ. Each person must repent of his or her sin and commit his or her life to Him, receiving Him as Lord and Savior.

Obviously, an infant can't do that. Certainly infant baptism or baby dedications can be a beautiful expression of a parent's commitment to raise a child in the ways of the Lord, but those ceremonies cannot make our kids Christians. That's a step each person—child or adult—must take for himself.

Years ago, someone coined a phrase to emphasize that point. He said, "God has no grandchildren." In one sense that's true. Every Christian is born again only through a direct and personal interaction with God. So, as believers, we are all His children—not His grandchildren.

In another sense, however, God actually does have grandchildren. He even has great-grandchildren. How can I say such a thing? Because the Bible says God has laid claim in advance to the sons and daughters, and grandsons and granddaughters of His people. He has reserved the right to bless them, protect them from evil, and draw their hearts to Himself, not because they personally asked Him to do it, but because their parents or grandparents did.

So in a way, God really does treat our descendents as if they are His grandchildren or great-grandchildren by extending the benefits of our covenant to them. That shouldn't surprise us. Ever since God began making covenants with mankind, He has included their children in those covenants. After the great flood recorded in Genesis 7, for instance, God said to Noah, *"Behold, I establish my covenant with you, **and with your seed after you**"* (Genesis 9:9 KJV, emphasis added). When God made covenant with Abraham, He said, *"I will establish my covenant between Me and you **and your descendants after you**"* (Genesis 17:7, emphasis added). When He reaffirmed that covenant to Abraham's grandson, Jacob, He said, *"[I will] give you the blessing of Abraham, to you and your descendants with you"* (Genesis 28:4).

Generations later, when God covenanted to bless the Israelites, He promised to bless their offspring as well. (See Deuteronomy 28:4 NASB.) Even when the Israelites rebelled against God, because of His covenant with them, God said He would continue to plead with them to return to Him, *"and with your children's children will I plead"* (Jeremiah 2:9 KJV).

In the New Testament, God continues His pattern of extending the benefits of His covenant to the descendants of His people by declaring that the children of believers are *"holy"* (1 Corinthians 7:14). The word *holy* translated from the Greek word *hagios* means "sacred or set apart for God's purposes." To those who are set apart for His purposes, God promises to draw our children into a personal relationship with Himself. In other words, He promises to save them.

In Deuteronomy 30:6, God confirmed that promise and said, *"The LORD your God will circumcise your heart and the heart of your descendants, to love the LORD your God with all your heart and with all your soul, that you may live.*" In Psalm 103, He confirmed it again and declared that "*the love of the* LORD *remains forever with those who fear him.* **His salvation extends to the children's children** *of those who are faithful to his covenant, of those who obey his commandments!*" (verses 17–18 NLT, emphasis added).

God doesn't just promise to save our children eternally and get them to heaven, either. He says He will teach them and speak to them all the days of their lives. He says to believing parents, "*My Spirit who is upon you, and My words which I have put in your mouth, shall not depart from your mouth, nor from the mouth of your descendants, nor from the mouth of your descendants' descendants…from this time and forevermore*" (Isaiah 59:21). He guarantees us that "*all your children shall be taught by the* LORD, *and great shall be the peace of your children*" (Isaiah 54:13).

During the battle over my son, Aaron, I meditated on those promises until I got such a strong grip on them that the devil himself couldn't wrench them away from me. I so imbedded them in my heart that I didn't even have to make a conscious effort to confess them. They practically flew out of my mouth of their own accord.

I'll never forget the moment I realized that nothing could make me doubt them. Some well-meaning friend was trying to talk some sense into me by reminding me that God would never violate a person's free will. "If Aaron chooses freely to reject God," she informed me, "then God will honor that choice no matter how fervently you pray."

The reply I fired back surprised even me. "If that's the case, I must assume that God, knowing the end from the beginning, gave me children who would freely choose to receive Him. Otherwise, He would have to break His Word to honor their free will. And God will never break His Word!"

That's the kind of rock-solid faith we require to pray effectively for our children. And since faith begins where the will of God is known, our first priority as parents must be to know and believe that it's God's will to save our kids. We must have no doubt that He has given us His Word that He will do so. Only then can we confidently claim our children for the kingdom of God.

And claim them we must! Otherwise, the devil will be free to move in on them. Like a squatter who illegally takes possession of someone else's property, he'll make our children's lives his playground until we come boldly to God's throne of grace and declare our scriptural rights. When we do that, God can release His full power on our behalf and kick the devil off our territory. When we exert our right of prior claim to our children—a right God has given to us in His Word—we open the door for Him to do whatever is necessary to sweep them out of the kingdom of darkness and into His light of His dear Son.

Sometimes the devil will contest our rights for a season. Sometimes, as we've seen, we have to stand in faith and fight in prayer to keep demonic forces from slamming that door shut again before God's work is done. But if we will do it, God guarantees us they will be saved…and there's not a thing the devil can do about it.

The Blessing— God's Greatest Gift

Once our children are born again, the Bible offers us even more good news about them. It tells us God will not only save them spiritually; He will bless them in other ways too. He will keep them safe. He will prosper them financially and protect them from lack. He will make them a mighty influence on the earth.

God's Word promises to do all those things for our children and more. It says:

I have been young, and now am old; yet I have not seen the righteous forsaken, nor his descendants begging bread.
(Psalm 37:25)

May the LORD *give you increase more and more, you and your children.*   (Psalm 115:14)

Who is the man that fears the LORD*? Him shall He teach in the way He chooses. He himself shall dwell in prosperity, and his descendants shall inherit the earth.*   (Psalm 25:12–13)

The children of your people will live in security. Their children's children will thrive in your presence.
(Psalm 102:28 NLT)

Happy are those who fear the LORD*. Yes, happy are those who delight in doing what he commands. Their children will be successful everywhere; an entire generation of godly people will be blessed.*   (Psalm 112:1–2 NLT)

Many believers today miss the power behind God's commitment to bless their children because they don't realize what the scriptural word translated "*blessing*" actually means. They don't know that a blessing is the greatest gift God can bestow. Translated from the Hebrew word *barak*, the word *blessing* means "to endue with power for success, prosperity, fruitfulness, and longevity."

Once our kids are born again and brought into a living relationship with God, what more could we ask for them than that they succeed in every area of life, prosper, be fruitful, and live long? All Christian parents want to see their children enjoy that kind of blessing. Most of us pray regularly toward that end. But our prayers will be more effective once we realize God has already promised to answer them. Once we are confident that our divine covenant extends to our children's children, we will be better equipped to help release God's blessing in our children's lives.

Teach Them How to Walk

Notice, I said we *help* release it. God never intended for us to carry our children on our faith alone for their entire lives. He planned for us to teach them how to walk with God and enter into the blessings of His covenant for themselves. He wants us to instruct them in His Word and His ways so they can eventually grow up and stand by faith on their own two feet.

If you want to know how important it is to God for us to do that, consider this: God chose Abraham to be the father of faith primarily because He could count on him to instruct his children in the ways of the Lord. God didn't call Abraham because he was especially bold or courageous. He didn't pick him because he was unusually gifted or spiritually sensitive. God said He chose Abraham because *"I know him, that he will command his children and his household after him, and they shall keep the way of the LORD"* (Genesis 18:19 KJV).

There's no question about it; God intends for all of us to follow Abraham's example. All through the Bible, He commands us to make teaching our children a priority in our lives. He tells us not only to put God's words in our own heart but to teach them diligently to our children, and talk of them when we sit in our house, when we walk by the way, when we lie down, and when we rise up...teach them to your children and your grandchildren. (See Deuteronomy 6:7, 4:9.)

Throughout the Scriptures, God urges us not to hide His truths from our kids but to make a practice of continually....

> *Telling to the generation to come the praises of the LORD, and His strength and His wonderful works that He has done. For He established a testimony in Jacob, and appointed a law in Israel, which He commanded our fathers, that they should make them known to their children; that the generation to come might know them, the children who would be born, that they may arise and declare them to their children, that they may set their hope in God, and not forget the works of God, but keep His commandments.* (Psalm 78:4–7)

> *Train up a child in the way he should go, and when he is old he will not depart from it.* (Proverbs 22:6)

Sometimes New Testament believers are tempted to neglect such instructions because they're in the Old Testament. But as born-again believers, we have a better covenant with God than the Old Covenant saints did, so we should be even more committed to teaching our children about it than they were. We should make full use of the power of the Holy Spirit and the anointing He has given us to teach our children everything we've learned about walking with God. We should devote ourselves wholly to bringing them up *"in the training and admonition of the Lord"* (Ephesians 6:4).

Be a Living Letter to Your Children

Some of the spiritual training we're to provide for our children is obvious. It almost goes without saying that as Christian parents, we are all responsible to teach our children what the Bible says. In every way possible—by reading it to them, talking to them about how it applies to their lives, taking them to church classes where they can hear it taught in a way they can understand—we should plant the seed of God's Word in their heart.

Once implanted within them, that Word will not only provide them with a mental understanding of God's ways, but it will also release the very power of God into their lives. That's because God's Word doesn't just convey information, it carries His very Spirit. As Hebrews 4:12 says, "*The Word of God is living and powerful, and sharper than any two-edged sword, piercing even to the division of soul and spirit, and of joints and marrow, and is a discerner of the thoughts and intents of the heart.*"

Once that Word is woven into our children's hearts, even if they want to forget it, the Holy Spirit will see to it they can't. He will bring it to their remembrance again...and again...and again. (See John 14:26.) He will ensure that it lives and abides in them forever. (See 1 Peter 1:23.)

As vital as it is that we tell our children what the Word says, however, showing them is even more important. Actions always speak louder than words, so the most powerful spiritual lessons our kids ever learn from us will be those we teach them by obeying God's Word ourselves.

We must always remember: Children learn best to pray not just by hearing what the Bible says about prayer, but by seeing their parents often upon their knees. Children learn how to be loving not just by memorizing the verse "*Be ye kind one to another,*" but by witnessing God's loving kindness demonstrated at home. Children grow up to be holy not just because they've been warned about the dangers of sin but because they have seen the beauty of purity in their parents' lives.

"But how can we set such an example?" you might ask. "How can we overcome our weaknesses and live the Word in such a way that our children can see and believe it?"

God will enable us by His grace. If we ask Him and trust Him to do it, He will anoint us with His own power and make us living letters from Himself to our kids.

That doesn't mean we'll be perfect and never make a mistake. It simply means that when we do make mistakes, we'll have the grace to acknowledge them and make things right. Sometimes that can send a more potent message to our kids than if we never made those mistakes at all.

I learned that difficult lesson one night when my daughter, during her teenage years, pressed my patience past the breaking point. What she did to provoke me is irrelevant now, so suffice it to say, I was quite righteously provoked. She had disobeyed my direct instructions and lied to me about it for no good reason. As a result, I lost my temper.

Storming into her room, scarlet-faced and wagging an accusing finger at her, I unloaded my wrath at high decibels untempered by kindness and with no affirmation of love. I was more concerned at that moment with my own hurt feelings than I was about helping guide her to a place of repentance and restoration. She had wounded my heart, so I purposely made her feel as small and ashamed as I could. Then I turned my back to her and marched out, the very image of self-righteousness.

A few minutes later, the conviction of the Holy Spirit descended—not upon her but upon me. Just imagine! He had the audacity to suggest that I was the one now who needed to go to her and ask for forgiveness, rather than the other way around.

"But Lord," I argued, "she was the one who did wrong. She disobeyed me! She lied to me!"

*That's true; and your responsibility was to respond to her dis-
obedience with loving discipline, not with disrespect and intemperate
wrath. You injured her instead of helping her. Now you owe her an
apology.*

Sometimes obeying the Lord is easy. Sometimes it's hard.
That night it was especially tough because I felt that by apologiz-
ing, I would make matters worse. Surely my daughter, who had
already treated me with such disrespect, would disrespect me
more for admitting I was wrong. Surely, if I put the spotlight of
blame on myself, her misbehavior would slip off into the darkness
unacknowledged.

That's how I saw it, anyway. But the Lord didn't seem concerned about my opinion; He just wanted my obedience, so I gave
it to Him.

I went back into my daughter's room and humbled myself
beneath her surly gaze. I told her I loved her and, although she had
disobeyed, I was wrong to be ugly and unkind to her. Then I asked
her to forgive me. She responded by shrugging her shoulders and
burying her face in a fashion magazine.

I didn't say it but I thought, *See, Lord? That didn't do any good
at all!*

The next morning, however, I found on my desk a letter
from my daughter, left there late the night before. "Dear Mom,"
she wrote, "I just want you to know there is no one in the world
I admire more than you. You don't just tell me about God's love,
you give it to me even when I know I don't deserve it. Please don't
worry about me. I won't always be a teenager. Someday I will grow
up, and I hope I will turn out to be a lot like you."

That's what God's promise to raise children can do; it can
teach you how to turn your mistakes into godly lessons your children will remember all their lives. It will give you the grace to do

things that might otherwise be impossible—all for the sake of the young ones you so dearly love.

Supernatural Solutions

If you're intimidated by the challenge of raising godly children in the midst of the ungodly culture that surrounds us these days and if you're afraid you won't know how to pray for them like you should or teach them all they need to know, you're not alone. Every Christian parent feels that way at one time or another because, on our own, we are all inadequate for the task.

Only God Himself is wise and powerful enough to shepherd the littlest lambs in His kingdom safely through the demonic minefields of our day. Certainly Bible-based parenting classes can teach us basic principles that will help us; but when we've finished the parenting workbook and completed all the classes, our kids will always come up with something the instructor didn't cover. And we'll find ourselves on our knees again asking God, "What on earth should I do?"

That's a question He will always answer. He will always lead us by His Spirit in the way that we, as parents, should go. If we will look to Him, He will give us supernatural solutions to the most perplexing problems. He will show us how to outsmart the devil every time.

That kind of wisdom is included in the power God provides for us, as parents. But to receive that wisdom, we must first dare to believe He will give it to us. We must put our faith in scriptural promises like these:

> *If any of you lacks wisdom, let him ask of God, who gives to all liberally and without reproach, and it will be given to him.*
>
> (James 1:5)

Trust in the LORD *with all your heart, and lean not on your own understanding; in all your ways acknowledge Him, and He shall direct your paths.*   (Proverbs 3:5–6)

Thus says the LORD *who made it, the* LORD *who formed it to establish it (the* LORD *is His name): "Call to Me, and I will answer you, and show you great and mighty things, which you do not know."*   (Jeremiah 33:2–3)

The Helper, the Holy Spirit, whom the Father will send in My name, He will teach you all things, and bring to your remembrance all things that I said to you.   (John 14:26)

All those promises apply to us, but the last one is especially relevant because Jesus made it directly to His disciples—not only to the first twelve listed in the New Testament, but to the rest of us as well. He knew we would encounter stormy situations we wouldn't know how to handle. He knew we'd need divine guidance to navigate our way through them. So He sent the Holy Spirit to live within us and teach us *all things*.

The problem is, we often forget to ask for the Holy Spirit's help. We fail to remember that He is present with us twenty-four hours a day, constantly ready and willing to release to us all the divine power and wisdom we need to become the best parents this world has ever seen. When we do remember, we're not always confident we can recognize and follow the Holy Spirit's leading. But we can develop that confidence by reminding ourselves that Jesus assured us that we, as believers, would *know and recognize* the Holy Spirit. He told us that we would have *close fellowship* with Him. (See John 14:17; 16:7 AMP). He promised us that *"when He, the Spirit of truth, has come, He will guide you into all truth"* (John 16:13).

Of course, we must seek that truth before we can find it. We must take the time to listen before we can hear. But if we will do those things in faith, the Holy Spirit will never let us down.

When my children were very young, I didn't understand that, so I often had to stumble along on my own. But I have a dear friend who developed her ability to follow the leading of the Holy Spirit in raising her kids from the time they were toddlers. My, what supernatural things He has shown her and done for her as a parent over the years!

I remember one particular time when her young son inexplicably began to steal things around the house. She initially tried to solve the problem as most of us would by confronting him. The confrontation, however, went miserably awry. Instead of confessing, her son set his jaw, shook his little blond head, and denied any knowledge of the missing items.

No doubt, my friend could have exerted enough parental pressure to force him into telling the truth; but she wasn't sure that was the best solution, so she asked the Lord to give her His wisdom about the situation. What He told her still amazes me.

Your son is not confident that the love you have for him is big enough to cover the wrong he has done, He said to her when she prayed. *That's why he won't be honest with you. If you will pray for him and reaffirm your love for him, everything will be all right.*

That day when her son came home from school, my friend followed the Lord's instructions. She clasped his small hand, pulled him close and began to pray for him. Since she is a charismatic Christian, she prayed first in other tongues at the direction of the Holy Spirit. As she did, her son stared up at her, his blue eyes wide and astonished. "Mom!" he said, "the words you just prayed are Spanish words that we've been studying in school. You were praying in Spanish about how much you love me!"

Wriggling free from her arms, he rushed upstairs to his room then thundered back down again moments later, his short legs pumping. In his hands, he clutched a shoe box filled with the items he had pilfered from the house. Confession was made, forgiveness was granted, and lying was never a significant problem in his life again.

Today that boy is a chaplain on his college campus. He teaches a Bible study in a place few people would expect to find one—a men's fraternity house. He shines like the morning star he was raised to be by a mother who discovered early what God's promise of protection for children can do.

Restoring the Years the Locusts Have Eaten

How marvelous it would be if every Christian parent had that revelation in the early years of their children's lives! What great victories we would see—both in our families and in the kingdom of God!

But many Christian parents don't find out about God's promises for their children until their kids are older. Many may even feel they learned about it too late. As I once did, they look at their wayward teenagers and grieve, wondering how different those young people might be if only they'd been taught the Bible and prayed for more diligently when they were younger. Some parents whose children have already grown up and left home—without being trained up, as the Bible says, in the way they should go— assume the opportunity they once had to bless those children has forever slipped away.

Yet, even for those parents, the Bible has a message of hope. It tells us that God is, above all, a God of redemption and restoration.

He is the God who once promised His people that despite their neglect of His Word, despite their ungodly past and the harm that came to them as a result of it, He would give them a glorious future. "*I will restore to you the years that the locust hath eaten,*" He said. "*And ye shall eat in plenty, and be satisfied, and praise the name of the* LORD *your God, that hath dealt wondrously with you: and my people shall never be ashamed*" (Joel 2:25–26 KJV).

If God would deal so wondrously with His Old Covenant servants, how much more graciously will He deal with us, as His New Covenant sons and daughters? Surely, He will pour out His power upon us and upon our children and restore to us what the devil has stolen. Even if our children are already grown...even if they have children of their own...our gracious heavenly Father will help us lay hold of His promises of blessing for them. He will still find a way to bring those promises to pass in their lives.

We might be tempted to wonder how such a thing could be possible. Can God truly help our children reach their divine destinies when so much time has been lost?

The Bible gives us the answer to that question.

"*With God all things are possible*" (Matthew 19:26).

If we will only believe that, God can keep the promises He has made to us about our children. Whether our children are toddlers or teenagers, infants or adults, He can woo them and win them to Himself. He can bless and protect them all the days of their life. He can send them forth as flaming arrows of righteousness to set the earth ablaze with the glory of God.

SCRIPTURES FOR
CHILDREN

SCRIPTURES FOR CHILDREN

Taken from the *New King James Version*

And as for Me, behold, I establish My covenant with you and with your descendants after you. (Genesis 9:9)

And I will establish My covenant between Me and you and your descendants after you in their generations, for an everlasting covenant, to be God to you and your descendants after you. (Genesis 17:7)

May God Almighty bless you, and make you fruitful and multiply you, that you may be an assembly of peoples; and give you the blessing of Abraham, to you and your descendants with you. (Genesis 28:3–4)

No one shall suffer miscarriage or be barren in your land; I will fulfill the number of your days. (Exodus 23:26)

*You shall be blessed above all peoples; there shall not be a male
or female barren among you or among your livestock.*

(Deuteronomy 7:14)

*Blessed shall be the fruit of your body, the produce of your
ground and the increase of your herds, the increase of your
cattle and the offspring of your flocks.*   (Deuteronomy 28:4)

*And the L*ORD *your God will circumcise your heart and the
heart of your descendants, to love the Lord your God with all
your heart and with all your soul, that you may live.*

(Deuteronomy 30:6)

*Blessed is the man who walks not in the counsel of the ungodly,
nor stands in the path of sinners, nor sits in the seat of the
scornful; but his delight is in the law of the L*ORD*, and in His
law he meditates day and night. He shall be like a tree planted
by the rivers of water, that brings forth its fruit in its season,
whose leaf also shall not wither; and whatever he does shall
prosper.*   (Psalm 1:1–3)

*I will both lie down in peace, and sleep; for You alone, O
L*ORD*, make me dwell in safety.*   (Psalm 4:8)

*The L*ORD *also will be a refuge for the oppressed, a refuge in
times of trouble.*   (Psalm 9:9)

*They are satisfied with children, and leave the rest of their
substance for their babes.*   (Psalm 17:14)

*He himself shall dwell in prosperity, and his descendants shall
inherit the earth.*   (Psalm 25:12–13)

I have been young, and now am old; yet I have not seen the righteous forsaken, nor his descendants begging bread.

(Psalm 37:25)

He will bring justice to the poor of the people; He will save the children of the needy, and will break in pieces the oppressor.

(Psalm 72:4)

Give ear, O my people, to my law; incline your ears to the words of my mouth. I will open my mouth in a parable; I will utter dark sayings of old, which we have heard and known, and our fathers have told us. We will not hide them from their children, telling to the generation to come the praises of the LORD, and His strength and His wonderful works that He has done.

(Psalm 78:1–4)

He who dwells in the secret place of the Most High shall abide under the shadow of the Almighty. I will say of the LORD, "He is my refuge and my fortress; My God, in Him I will trust." Surely He shall deliver you from the snare of the fowler and from the perilous pestilence. He shall cover you with His feathers, and under His wings you shall take refuge; His truth shall be your shield and buckler. You shall not be afraid of the terror by night, nor of the arrow that flies by day, nor of the pestilence that walks in darkness, nor of the destruction that lays waste at noonday. A thousand may fall at your side, and ten thousand at your right hand; but it shall not come near you. Only with your eyes shall you look, and see the reward of the wicked. Because you have made the LORD, who is my refuge, even the Most High, your habitation, no evil shall befall you, nor shall any plague come near your dwelling; for He shall give His angels charge over you, to keep you in all your ways. They shall bear you up in their hands, lest you dash your foot against a stone. You shall tread upon the lion and the cobra, the young lion and the serpent you shall trample under foot. Because he has set his love upon Me, therefore I will deliver him; I will set him on high, because he has known My name. He shall call upon Me, and I will answer him; I will be with him in trouble; I will deliver him and honor him. With long life I will satisfy him, and show him My salvation.

(Psalm 91)

They shall still bear fruit in old age; they shall be fresh and flourishing.　　　　　　　　　　　　　　(Psalm 92:14)

But the mercy of the Lord *is from everlasting to everlasting on those who fear Him, and His righteousness to children's children, to such as keep His covenant, and to those who remember His commandments to do them.*

(Psalm 103:17–19)

His descendants will be mighty on earth; the generation of the upright will be blessed.　　　　　　　　　(Psalm 112:2)

He grants the barren woman a home, like a joyful mother of children. Praise the Lord!　　　　　　　　(Psalm 113:9)

Behold, children are a heritage from the Lord, *the fruit of the womb is His reward.*　　　　　　　　　(Psalm 127:3)

Like arrows in the hand of a warrior, so are the children of one's youth. Happy is the man who has his quiver full of them; they shall not be ashamed, but shall speak with their enemies in the gate.　　　　　　　　　　　　(Psalm 127:4–5)

Your wife shall be like a fruitful vine in the very heart of your house, your children like olive plants all around your table.
(Psalm 128:3)

Yes, may you see your children's children.   (Psalm 128:6)

For He has strengthened the bars of your gates; He has blessed your children within you.   (Psalm 147:13)

Trust in the Lord with all your heart, and lean not on your own understanding; in all your ways acknowledge Him, and He shall direct your paths.   (Proverbs 3:5–6)

Get wisdom! Get understanding! Do not forget, nor turn away from the words of my mouth. Do not forsake her, and she will preserve you; love her, and she will keep you. Wisdom is the principal thing; therefore get wisdom. And in all your getting, get understanding.   (Proverbs 4:5–7)

Hear, my son, and receive my sayings, and the years of your life will be many. I have taught you in the way of wisdom; I have led you in right paths. When you walk, your steps will not be hindered, and when you run, you will not stumble.
(Proverbs 9:10–12)

The righteous should choose his friends carefully, for the way of the wicked leads them astray.   (Proverbs 12:26)

In the fear of the LORD there is strong confidence, and His children will have a place of refuge.   (Proverbs 14:26)

Though they join forces, the wicked will not go unpunished; but the posterity of the righteous will be delivered.
(Proverbs 11:21)

The fear of the Lord is a fountain of life, to avoid the snares of death. (Proverbs 14:27)

Children's children are the crown of old men, and the glory of children is their father. (Proverbs 17:6)

The righteous man walks in his integrity; his children are blessed after him. (Proverbs 20:7)

A wise man is strong, yes, a man of knowledge increases strength; for by wise counsel you will wage your own war, and in a multitude of counselors there is safety.
(Proverbs 22:5–6)

Make no friendship with an angry man, and with a furious man do not go, lest you learn his ways and set a snare for your soul. (Proverbs 22:24–25)

Her children rise up and call her blessed; her husband also, and he praises her. (Proverbs 31:28)

Here am I and the children whom the LORD has given me! (Isaiah 8:18)

The Spirit of the LORD shall rest upon Him, the Spirit of wisdom and understanding, the Spirit of counsel and might, the Spirit of knowledge and of the fear of the LORD. His delight is in the fear of the LORD, and He shall not judge by the sight of His eyes, nor decide by the hearing of His ears.
(Isaiah 11:2–3)

Fear not, for I am with you; be not dismayed, for I am your God. I will strengthen you, yes, I will help you, I will uphold you with My righteous right hand.   (Isaiah 41:10)

When you pass through the waters, I will be with you; and through the rivers, they shall not overflow you. When you walk through the fire, you shall not be burned, nor shall the flame scorch you.   (Isaiah 43:2)

But thus says the Lord: *"Even the captives of the mighty shall be taken away, and the prey of the terrible be delivered; for I will contend with him who contends with you, and I will save your children."*   (Isaiah 49:25)

"Sing, O barren, you who have not borne! Break forth into singing, and cry aloud, you who have not travailed with child! For more are the children of the desolate than the children of the married woman," says the Lord.   (Isaiah 54:1)

All your children shall be taught by the Lord, *and great shall be the peace of your children.*   (Isaiah 54:13)

In righteousness you shall be established; you shall be far from oppression, for you shall not fear; and from terror, for it shall not come near you.   (Isaiah 54:14)

No weapon formed against you shall prosper, and every tongue which rises against you in judgment you shall condemn. This is the heritage of the servants of the Lord, *and their righteousness is from Me," says the* Lord.   (Isaiah 54:17)

They shall not labor in vain, nor bring forth children for trouble; for they shall be the descendants of the blessed of the LORD, *and their offspring with them.*   (Isaiah 65:23)

For since the beginning of the world men have not heard nor perceived by the ear, nor has the eye seen any God besides You, who acts for the one who waits for Him.   (Isaiah 63:4)

Before I formed you in the womb I knew you; before you were born I sanctified you; and I ordained you a prophet to the nations.   (Jeremiah 1:5)

Thus says the LORD: *"Refrain your voice from weeping, and your eyes from tears; for your work shall be rewarded," says the* LORD, *"and they shall come back from the land of the enemy. There is hope in your future," says the* LORD, *"that your children shall come back to their own border."*
        (Jeremiah 31:16–17)

Call to Me, and I will answer you, and show you great and mighty things, which you do not know.   (Jeremiah 33:3)

For I know the thoughts that I think toward you, says the LORD, *thoughts of peace and not of evil, to give you a future and a hope.*   (Jeremiah 29:11)

They shall be My people, and I will be their God; then I will give them one heart and one way, that they may fear Me forever, for the good of them and their children after them. And I will make an everlasting covenant with them, that I will not turn away from doing them good; but I will put My fear in their hearts so that they will not depart from Me.
        (Jeremiah 32:38–40)

So I will restore to you the years that the swarming locust has eaten, the crawling locust, the consuming locust, and the chewing locust.   (Joel 2:26)

And it shall come to pass afterward that I will pour out My Spirit on all flesh; your sons and your daughters shall prophesy, your old men shall dream dreams, your young men shall see visions; and also on My menservants and on My maidservants I will pour out My Spirit in those days.

(Joel 2:28–29)

If you then, being evil, know how to give good gifts to your children, how much more will your Father who is in heaven give good things to those who ask Him!   (Matthew 7:11)

Therefore do not fear them. For there is nothing covered that will not be revealed, and hidden that will not be known.

(Matthew 10:26)

But I say to you that for every idle word men may speak, they will give account of it in the day of judgment. For by your words you will be justified, and by your words you will be condemned.   (Matthew 12:36–37)

Again I say to you that if two of you agree on earth concerning anything that they ask, it will be done for them by My Father in heaven. For where two or three are gathered together in My name, I am there in the midst of them.

(Matthew 18:19–20)

And I will give you the keys of the kingdom of heaven, and whatever you bind on earth will be bound in heaven, and whatever you loose on earth will be loosed in heaven.

(Matthew 16:19)

For assuredly, I say to you, whoever says to this mountain, "Be removed and be cast into the sea," and does not doubt in his heart, but believes that those things he says will come to pass, he will have whatever he says. Therefore I say to you, whatever things you ask when you pray, believe that you receive them, and you will have them.   (Mark 11:23–24)

And whenever you stand praying, if you have anything against anyone, forgive him, that your Father in heaven may also forgive you your trespasses.   (Mark 11:25)

For God so loved the world that He gave His only begotten Son, that whoever believes in Him should not perish but have everlasting life.   (John 3:16)

Peace I leave with you, My peace I give to you; not as the world gives do I give to you. Let not your heart be troubled, neither let it be afraid.   (John 14:22)

And it shall come to pass in the last days, says God, that I will pour out of My Spirit on all flesh; your sons and your daughters shall prophesy, your young men shall see visions, your old men shall dream dreams. And on My menservants and on My maidservants I will pour out My Spirit in those days; and they shall prophesy.   (Acts 2:17–18)

Likewise the Spirit also helps in our weaknesses. For we do not know what we should pray for as we ought, but the Spirit Himself makes intercession for us with groanings which cannot be uttered. Now He who searches the hearts knows what the mind of the Spirit is, because He makes intercession for the saints according to the will of God.

(Romans 8:26–27)

And do not be conformed to this world, but be transformed by the renewing of your mind, that you may prove what is that good and acceptable and perfect will of God.
(Romans 12:2)

Now may the God of hope fill you with all joy and peace in believing, that you may abound in hope by the power of the Holy Spirit. (Romans 15:13)

And the God of peace will crush Satan under your feet shortly. The grace of our Lord Jesus Christ be with you.
(Romans 16:20)

For the weapons of our warfare are not carnal but mighty in God for pulling down strongholds, casting down arguments and every high thing that exalts itself against the knowledge of God, bringing every thought into captivity to the obedience of Christ. (2 Corinthians 10:4–5)

And be kind to one another, tenderhearted, forgiving one another, just as God in Christ also forgave you.
(Ephesians 4:32)

Be anxious for nothing, but in everything by prayer and supplication, with thanksgiving, let your requests be made known to God; and the peace of God, which surpasses all understanding, will guard your hearts and minds through Christ Jesus.
(Philippians 4:6–7)

For the word of God is living and powerful, and sharper than any two-edged sword, piercing even to the division of soul and spirit, and of joints and marrow, and is a discerner of the thoughts and intents of the heart. (Hebrews 4:12)

If any of you lacks wisdom, let him ask of God, who gives to all liberally and without reproach, and it will be given to him.

(James 1:5)

ABOUT THE AUTHORS

ABOUT THE AUTHORS

Melanie Hemry

A former intensive care nurse, Melanie Hemry traded in her stethoscope for a computer and now writes poignant true life stories, many of which are set in intensive care. A 1988 winner of the coveted *Guideposts* Writing Contest, Melanie's stories have warmed the hearts of readers around the world. She holds a bachelor of science in nursing from the University of Central Oklahoma and a master's degree in Practical Ministry from Wagner Leadership Institute in Colorado Springs. She is the author of *A Healing Touch*. Melanie and her husband, Ken, are the parents of two grown daughters, Heather and Lauren, and they reside in Edmond, Oklahoma.

Gina Lynnes

A writer by trade and a minister at heart, Gina Lynnes has been a Bible teacher and associate pastor since 1996, ministering especially on the subject of prayer in churches both in the Unites States and abroad. A recipient of the National Religious Broadcasters award for her writing of the *UpReach!* Radio broadcast, she has been involved in Christian publishing for more than twenty years, working behind the scenes as a writer and editor for a number of international ministries. Gina and her husband, Kelly, pastor a church in Littleton, Colorado, where they now reside.